P9-BIW-764

The Philosophy of Hegel

Seventeen of the most important
books on Hegel's philosophy
reprinted in sixteen volumes

Edited by
H. S. Harris
York University

A GARLAND SERIES

Hegel's Hellenic Ideal

J. Glenn Gray

The Mystical Element in Hegel's Early Theological Writings

George Plimpton Adams

Garland Publishing, Inc.
New York & London
1984

For a complete list of the titles in this series
see the final pages of this volume.

The facsimile of *Hegel's Hellenic Ideal* has
been made from a copy in the Yale Divinity
School Library, that of the *Mystical Element in
Hegel's Early Theological Writings* is from
the Yale University Library.

Library of Congress Cataloging in Publication Data

Gray, J. Glenn (Jesse Glenn), 1913–1977.
Hegel's Hellenic ideal.

(The Philosophy of Hegel)
Reprint (1st work). Originally published: New York :
King's Crown Press, 1941.
Reprint (2nd work). Originally published: Berkeley :
University Press, 1910, as vol. 2, no. 4, p. 67–102 of
University of California publications in philosophy.
Includes bibliographies and index.
1. Hegel, Georg Wilhelm Friedrich, 1770–1831.
2. Hellenism. I. Adams, George Plimpton, 1882–1961.
Mystical element in Hegel's early theological writings.
1984. II. Title. III. Title: Mystical element in
Hegel's early theological writings. IV. Series.
B2948.G7 1984 193 83-48507
ISBN 0-8240-5630-2 (alk. paper)

63,291

The volumes in this series are printed on
acid-free, 250-year-life paper.

Printed in the United States of America

HEGEL'S HELLENIC IDEAL

CAMROSE LUTHERAN COLLEGE
LIBRARY

HEGEL'S HELLENIC IDEAL

By J. Glenn Gray

KING'S CROWN PRESS
MORNINGSIDE HEIGHTS · NEW YORK
1941

Copyright, 1941, by
J. GLENN GRAY

PRINTED IN THE UNITED STATES OF AMERICA

ZI

King's Crown Press is a division of Columbia University Press organized for the purpose of making certain scholarly material available at minimum cost. Toward that end, the publishers have adopted every reasonable economy except such as would interfere with a legible format. The work is presented substantially as submitted by the author, without the usual editorial and typographical attention of Columbia University Press.

TABLE OF CONTENTS

PREFACE

As an original and profound critic of our cultural heritage Hegel should not be neglected. His lectures on the interpretation of history, art, religion and the history of philosophy contain an astounding wealth of ideas that cannot be set aside as the bygone products of a dry encyclopedism or the a priori categories of a romantic logic. When the exclusive emphasis on his metaphysical system gives place to a more dispassionate evaluation of his historical insights, readers will turn to him to learn what he has to teach rather than to become partisan as Hegelians or as anti-Hegelians.

I have here undertaken to review the values which Hegel considered preeminently characteristic of Greek culture, and to trace the way in which these values helped to determine his judgment of modern civilization. To a great extent his personal and philosophical ideas and ideals grew out of his historical studies for which the classical period furnished the major material. I have followed his attempt to understand and to characterize for his students the peculiar significance of the Greek contribution to history, particularly its meaning for his own age. Hegel's understanding of classical culture necessarily suffered from the limitations of knowledge and methods of research of his time. Ethnologists and historians have since then enlarged our understanding of the Greeks by providing a greater factual basis for the interpretation of their culture. But in the present work my interest has not been in factual discrepancies; it concerns the philosophical wisdom which lies behind much that Hegel said about the Greeks.

The permanent value of German idealism consists in its poetic apprehension of empirical phenomena, its artistic appreciation and religious insight. The idealistic school was preoccupied with the meaning of events, with their relevance to human experience, not with recording and interpreting facts. The metaphysical systems in which Hegel and his contemporaries cast their thought may well be called philosophical mythologies. Their claim was not to describe empirical phenomena, but to comprehend in creative vision the meaning of the world, natural, human and divine. These systems are true, not in the sense that a scientific formula is true, but as a work of art is true. They represent the same kind of truth as does Dante's *Divine Comedy*. The idealists held that such truth is ultimately the only valuable truth, because it alone aims at setting for life a standard that satisfies the human spirit. Whatever may have been their illusions, these German idealists were subtle and profound enough to realize the symbolical character of their attempts to interpret the scope and deepest reach of man's surmise regarding his world.

The inevitable dogmatizing of these systems by a too literal-minded posterity has led to a natural reaction and has produced a distaste from which we have hardly yet escaped. As a burnt child dreads the fire, so the older generation has kept at a safe distance from all idealism. Now, however, it is time to return to these German thinkers and to read them not for their imposing metaphysics but for their cultural criticism, their artistic insight, their enduring wisdom. Hegel, who is unquestionably one of the greatest, requires today a thorough re-examination and reinterpretation. I hope that this short study may be a step in that direction.

My warm thanks are due to Professor Horace L. Friess of Columbia University who supervised and greatly assisted my study. I also wish to express my sense of obligation to Professor J. H. Randall, Jr., to whose instruction and suggestion I am indebted for many of the ideas which are here set forth. To Dr. Ida W. Kubitz of Juniata College in Pennsylvania I am especially grateful for help in acquainting me with the nature of the German literary genius. My friends at Pendle Hill have kindly assisted in revising the manuscript and in checking the proof. A generous grant from the National Council on Religion in Higher Education, of which I am a Fellow, has facilitated the publication of the monograph at this time.

Pendle Hill, Pennsylvania

I

HEGEL'S VISION OF HISTORY

Hegel's vision of history was permeated with a sense of the pathos of human experience. Throughout his many volumes innumerable passages reveal the sadness of a mind that had contemplated the record of the past with a fervor like that of actual participation. His was a keen, almost tragic insight into the picture of change and decay, the episodical nature of all careers in time, and it was his own need, ethical and religious, that impelled him through a lifetime to appraise the transient and finite character of human life and civilizations. History regarded as a spectacle was not self-explanatory; as drama it contained insufficient meaning to satisfy. An unforgettable paragraph in the *Philosophy of History* describes this record of mankind as the conflict of myriads of selfish interests.

When we look at this display of passions, and the consequences of their violence; the unreason which is associated not only with them, but even (rather we might say *especially*) with *good* designs and righteous aims; when we see the evil, the vice, the ruin that has befallen the most flourishing kingdoms which the mind of man ever created; we can scarce avoid being filled with sorrow at this universal taint of corruption. And, since this decay is not the work of mere Nature, but of the human will—a moral embitterment—a revolt of the good spirit (if it have a place within us) may well be the result of our reflections. Without rhetorical exaggeration, a simply truthful combination of the miseries that have overwhelmed the noblest of nations and polities, and the finest exemplars of private virtue—forms a picture of most fearful aspect, and excites emotions of the profoundest and most hopeless sadness, counterbalanced by no consolatory result. We endure in beholding it a mental torture, allowing no defence or escape but the consideration that what has happened could not be otherwise; that it is a fatality which no intervention could alter. And at last we draw back from the intolerable disgust with which these sorrowful reflections threaten us, into the more agreeable environment of our individual life—the Present formed by our private aims and interests. In short we retreat into the selfishness that stands on the quiet shore, and thence enjoys in safety the distant spectacle of "wrecks confusedly hurled."[1]

Though other men, appalled by this tragic drama, may retreat into the

The notes for this work will be discovered on page 95.

comfort of private and petty interests, this course is hardly possible for the philosopher. Men of intellectual strength must turn again to the larger world to seek for its meaning and truth. Hegel found the answer to despair in a great philosophical faith which defied the meaninglessness of history. It was the faith that the course of events was not governed mainly by accident and chance, but that it presented an essential continuity and pattern of development. History, he said, might well be regarded as the "slaughter-bench at which the happiness of peoples, the wisdom of states, and the virtue of individuals have been victimized". Nevertheless, as a thinker whose reflections were directed to the social and ethical archives of civilizations, Hegel felt impelled to ask to what purpose and to what final principle that record is directed.

As he contemplated the past, he found a partial answer in the fact that though death is the issue of life, life is also the issue of death. Peoples fall, ideals decay, but new nations and new ideals take their places. The age-old secret of natural life, which Hegel held to be the highest apprehension of the Eastern mind, is just this inextinguishable power of generation, the birth of the young from the old. He compared the vitality in history to the myth of the Phoenix, that prepares its own funeral pyre on which it is consumed, and lo! from the ashes there emerges a new Phoenix with life fresh and renewed. If history is a record of dissolution and death, it is no less a record of rebirth and of new beginnings.

But that was not enough for Hegel's vision. Mind or spirit, the distinctive element in man, was for him more than a Phoenix arising rejuvenated from the ashes. The myth described only the life of nature in which there is eternal repetition, an eternal sameness of individual forms. But human life, in so far as it is the life of spirit, is more than that. Men are more than sparrows. Mind proceeds into higher and more exalted forms; for it the past is not lost, but is used as the means to attain more adequate life. To the consideration of the universality of change, Hegel felt impelled to add the certainty of progress. This was the basis of his philosophy of history.

> The only thought which philosophy brings with it to the contemplation of history is the simple conception of *Reason*; that reason is the sovereign of the world; that the history of the world, therefore, presents us with a rational process.[2]

By reason, Hegel understood not merely an aspect of the individual mind, but also a characteristic structure in the objective social world, an intelligibility and order comparable to the laws of the physical world. For him mind was a continuity, and reason was a process of becoming more explicit at higher levels. Viewed then as a continuity of mind, history was a comprehensive teleological process, deriving essential unity from its inclusive end or goal which was human freedom. The history of the race presented a development according to inner law that determined its course, not in incidental and minor phases, but in essential movement—a progressive realization of ideal goals. On this point Hegel accepted the conviction of Lessing, Kant, and Herder.[3] This was a faith that saved from despair, and gave philosophy its unique significance. As a modern thinker he could not take literally the hope of Christian transcendentalism which found the meaning of history beyond the human sphere. He required that events contain their own justification. Reason as teleological continuity and process supplied this need for the interpretation of the past and present. It became for him a primary presupposition, a plausible intuition, essentially a philosophical faith.

This category of reason determined for Hegel what is essential and what is unessential, what is real in a permanent sense and what is merely empirically existent. He conceived it to be his task as a philosopher to understand the course of truly significant events and to relate less relevant particulars. Though he has often been justly attacked from the empirico-historical standpoint for approaching history with an a priori theory and for forcing the facts to fit the theory, it is more correct to say that his intention was not to force facts, but to account for them in the light of higher rational purposes. He claimed that the rational is determined as the valuable if one seeks to understand events in the light of reason. "To him who looks upon the world rationally, the world in its turn presents a rational aspect. The relation is mutual."[4]

If one accepts such a faith in the ultimate and long term rationality of human affairs, the question arises: How can reason account for and explain events? We meet in history more than the intelligible and the rational. Hegel answers: Yes, there is also passion (Leidenschaft). Passion, understood as the energy of will on the part of individuals in pursuit of personal, selfish aims, furnishes the driving force of history. According to Hegel, the actions of men proceed from their needs, passions, characters and talents. These natural impulses, the desire for self-realization on the part of all creatures, what Aristotle called *orexis*, attain their power and energy because they have scant respect for the "tedious discipline" of morality and justice.

Thus for Hegel all vital activity was first of all personal, private activity. For the men of the Enlightenment who spoke of pure, disinterested service of mankind, of doing the good for the sake of the good alone, Hegel had only scorn. He felt that such ideals were not founded on sound knowledge of human nature, nor were they needed for the acceptance or acknowledgment of a final universal goal.

> If I am to exert myself [he wrote] for any object, it must in some way or other be *my* object. In the accomplishment of such or such designs, I must at the same time find *my* satisfaction; although the purpose for which I exert myself includes a complication of results, many of which have no interest for me. This is the absolute right of personal existence— to find *itself* satisfied in its activity and labour. If men are to interest themselves for anything, they must, so to speak, have part of their existence involved in it; find their individuality gratified by its attainment.[5]

Hence to fail to take account of the personal motivation behind all action is to miss the whole meaning of events in time. "Two elements, therefore, enter into the object of our investigation, the first the idea, the second, the complex of human passions; the one the warp, the other the woof of the vast arras-web of universal history."[6] By the idea, Hegel understood the all-encompassing reason, the teleological structure that was realizing itself in the process of history. By passion, conceived in its wider sense, he meant human activity resulting from private interests. These two, idea and passion, furnish the material for the philosopher of history; their relationship and interdependence is his problem. Hegel's philosophy of history is an attempt to grasp this relationship, to see in particular interests and activities the achievement of universal rational goals.

On the one hand, he seems to have regarded interdependence as a kind of end or result of particular activity. In spite of the fact that all action is selfish and all satisfaction personal, their final results fall outside the particular and achieve universal significance. These results, Hegel tells us, are not incidental, they are the very substance of reason itself, which works through determinate means to attain general ends. The individual is directed by forces larger than he knows. Sometimes Hegel used mythological language to describe this aspect of the relationship of the personal to the general. The tendency of reason not to reveal itself or expose itself in the conflicts of particular desires he called "the cunning of reason". Reason directs the passions, "puts them to work for itself", while remaining in the background "untouched and uninjured". In accordance with natural tendencies, men build up the edifice of society, establishing rules and laws by which to gratify personal aims, while at the same time they are "fortifying a position for right and order against themselves". In the congeries of conflicting interests and activities there remains an inner rational core that signifies development. For though the agents of activity have only limited and special aims, they are thinking beings, and, said Hegel, "the purpose of their desires is interwoven with general, essential considerations of justice, good, duty." These are precisely the rational content, the product of the idea, the goal of history.

On the other hand, Hegel saw the relationship of reason and passion from the standpoint of the whole. Behind all contradiction and the dualism of private passion and universal reason lay the motive power of the whole, which only the limitations of human sight conceal. Particular passions are blind, but passion as an integral part of the all-inclusive whole is at one with the world-reason—the developing, maturing plan of the world, which Hegel sometimes called God's Providence and at other times, Necessity. From this point of view reason and passion are not set over against each other; they are different aspects of the same thing. Reason is not merely a product, a non-vital end, but concurrent with the motive power of history. This relation can best be seen in concrete social and ethical terms by investigating the Hegelian conception of freedom.

That freedom is the goal toward which the teleological process of human history is directed, Hegel calmly asserted. To understand what he meant by that fine but ambiguous term, freedom, is to grasp an essential tenet of his philosophy. The relation between reason and passion runs parallel to the relation between the higher right of the group and the lower right of the individual. Universal history, as the record of the incorporation of values in reality, is essentially concerned with the question of freedom. This question Hegel attempted to answer in his analysis of the relationship of the individual and his environment, of the subjective and the objective.

To be free as an individual is, according to him, to overcome the primarily dualistic relationship existing between the ego and the objective world. He best achieves freedom who makes himself most completely at home in his world. To be free is to divest the outer and objective realm of its strangeness, its opposition to the self, its foreign character, and to find in it an adequate spiritual home. To be free is to see in the social world the reflection of one's own substance, the actualization of what the individual could most fully desire. Seen in this light, freedom is the progressive achievement of man's complete adjustment to his environment, to the world of his fellow men, to his nation and its past. If one were able to state this fundamental theme of Hegel's philosophy in a phrase or two, it might be expressed in this way: wisdom's final word is the recognition that man's good lies in finding his powers realized and himself at home in the objective world. Such satisfaction ought not to be the result of a resigned submission to external powers and traditions, but an acknowledgment and penetration of the objective world. Freedom lies in a voluntary, not a submissive, peace with reality.

This orientation of the individual in his world involves a continuous advance in self-consciousness. Self-consciousness, from Hegel's point of view, meant movement toward the objective, not a retreat within the self nor an antithesis with the outer. Freedom developed along with greater awareness, with widened horizons, with recognition of more inclusive unities in the social and spiritual realms. Freedom as self-consciousness signified advance from the subjective to the public, from the isolated to the implicated. Kinship between the self and its world, in its ideal possibility, was suggested by Hegel through the myth of our first parents. Adam looking upon Eve said: Thou art flesh of my flesh and bone of my bone. Antithesis is here ideally transcended and man is wholly free.

Such orientation, Hegel believed, could come only by knowledge, by the power of understanding and wisdom. Through education the individual becomes aware of spiritual bonds that unite man with the social institutions that give him life. To be educated is to be free. This liberating education is not so much the acquirement of technical skills as it is training in wisdom. It puts at man's disposal the experience of the race in the realms of art, morality, politics, religion and philosophy.

Hence for Hegel freedom was, first of all, intellectual awareness on the part of the individual of his place in the scheme of things. No philosopher has had greater confidence in the power of the mind than he. It is the prime article of his faith that the truth which frees is knowable. To be completely at home in the world is ideally possible through the power of intellect to participate wholly in truth.

> The love of truth, faith in the power of mind, is the first condition in philosophy. Man, because he is mind, should and must deem himself worthy of the highest. He cannot think too highly of the greatness and the power of his mind, and, with this belief, nothing will be so difficult and hard that it will not reveal itself to him. The being of the universe, at first hidden and concealed, has no power which can offer resistance to the search for knowledge; it has to lay itself open before the seeker—to set before his eyes and give for his enjoyment, its riches and depths.[7]

The conflict between the subjective and the objective, between reason and passion, is overcome by larger intellectual awareness. Tensions are resolved when man becomes conscious of the larger whole, when he sees freedom in terms of universal law rather than subjective caprice. Rationality of the world process is furthered when the individual learns through ripened wisdom to obtain the object of his passions by concentration upon general aims.

Only that will which obeys law, is free; for it obeys itself—it is independent and so free. When the state or our country constitutes a community of existence; when the subjective will of man submits to laws— the contradiction between liberty and necessity vanishes. The rational has necessary existence, as being the reality and substance of things, and we are free in recognizing it as law, and following it as the substance of our being.[8]

Hegel realized that such recognition is not, strictly speaking, natural to man. Freedom is farthest from a state of innocence. True liberty involves rebirth; it is a "second nature". The words which Jesus spoke to Nicodemus illustrate Hegel's doctrine not merely in a limited religious sense but also as applied to the whole of life in society. Man in his first nature is only potentially different from the animal. His actual humanity lies in the possibility of development, in rebirth into the intellectual, the spiritual. That can come only with gradual initiation into the established life of society. Until the developing individual arrives through a process of moral discipline at a reconciliation with the objective ethical order, he cannot actualize the potentiality of freedom.

This conception of freedom as man's finding himself at home in the world through reconciliation and rebirth brings us to another basic element in Hegel's philosophy of history, the concept of dialectic. Freedom as reconciliation involves conflict, estrangement, renunciation. Hegel's philosophy is built on the proposition that striving is the very life of the spirit. He beheld nature in contrast with spirit as the realm of the organic unfolding of life in what might be called a linear process. In nature the organism moves from the potential to the actual in a necessary and characteristic pattern. Movement and growth are part of its essential character, but they are relatively harmonious and continuous. Life of the spirit is also essentially movement and growth. Activity, said Hegel, is spirit's essence, its beginning and also its end. But spirit must be sharply differentiated from the natural organism, because spirit adds to organic unfolding dialectical movement.

Progress toward freedom, the actuality of spirit, Hegel described as movement between opposite poles. In the individual, life moves forward by opposition and contradiction. Man is able not only to compass conflicting principles within himself but also to endure them, to profit by them, to harmonize and reconcile them. Periods of happiness in individual existence are not periods of growth. Without pain and estrangement, without struggle and despair, there can be no worthy triumph.

> That which remains always affirmative is, and remains, without life. Life is built upon negation and pain. It is only by crushing out such contradictions in the crucible of fuller life and knowledge that it remains in its affirmative substance.[9]

Hegel sought to understand progress as the rhythm of a constant self-transcending. The life of the human spirit is a restless, never-ending evolvement. Hindrances and opposition are not outside but within the spirit. They are part of its essence. The spirit becomes estranged from itself. It is divided and becomes reconciled. The following passage summarizes this dialectical movement in figurative language.

> Thus spirit is at war with itself; it has to overcome itself as its most formidable obstacle. That development which in the sphere of nature is a peaceful growth, is in that of spirit, a severe, a mighty conflict with itself. What spirit really strives for is the realization of its ideal being; but in doing so it hides that goal from its own vision, and is proud and well satisfied in this alienation from it. Its expansion, therefore, does not present the harmless tranquillity of mere growth, as does that of organic life, but a stern reluctant working against itself. It exhibits, moreover, not the mere formal conception of development, but the attainment of a more definite result. The goal of attainment we determined at the outset: it is spirit in its *completeness*, in its essential nature, i.e. Freedom.[10]

Who are the combatants in this war? For what is the battle? Hegel would answer: It is the struggle to overcome the immediate, the unreflective, the purely natural. Man is first of all animal. He possesses the same sensuous needs, the same impulses and instincts as the sub-human species. But the wide gulf separating him from the animal is self-consciousness. The animal has no possibility of becoming conscious of itself, hence no possibility of controlling its immediate, instinctive needs and their satisfaction. But man, as a creature of reason and will, can overcome and master this primary nature. He can direct his life according to the higher laws of self-consciousness. His destiny is to pass beyond the immediacy of natural existence to the second nature of self-awareness. Development in man signifies this progress in rationality. The victory of spirit is conquest over itself for the attainment of new levels of reflective consciousness.

Hegel described the movement of the dialectical process in spirit as a triad. The first level is that of immediate unity or identity in which the spirit is at one with itself in its unreflective character. This first stage of unity is partial and incomplete; a latent disunion persists within it. Such disunion eventually comes to an open break. This is the level of contradiction and dualism which Hegel called the state of otherness. As a result of the struggle and estrangement a higher unity is born, and synthesis becomes in its turn a point of departure for a new dissension and a still higher reconciliation. Such is the growth and expansion of the spiritual life. Hegel maintained that the process is not to be understood as a pointless and eternal repetition, but as a purposeful and rational progress along the way toward autonomy and freedom.

However, it would be utterly wrong to think of this analysis of human life in exclusively individual terms. The activity of spirit as an organic unfolding by the dialectical process was for Hegel first and foremost a social phenomenon. The great compulsion, the duty of all life, is to make objective that which is within. The life of the individual flows into and flows from the life of society. The idea of the objective nature of values is basic in Hegel's thought. In his philosophy the social is the ultimate point of reference in relation to which the individual gains life and purpose. Human institutions are conceived as the product and concrete realization of this second nature of man. They are the expression of rebirth into the objective mind.

It is not enough to say that Hegel was upholding the classical idea of freedom as individual awareness of rationality. As we have seen, he also stressed social participation. To be free, to be reborn, man must turn to the objective world; the individual must participate in the practical or the ideal activities of society. The spirit can only be realized in terms of the varied cultural manifestations of a people's life. To the Romantic emphasis on individual inwardness Hegel opposed the doctrine that unless the inner life issues in actual fruits, it is empty and bare and futile. "All knowledge and learning, science, and even commerce have no other object than to draw out what is inward or implicit and thus to become objective."

History, the progress of the realization of freedom, became for Hegel the history of peoples, of social wholes and cultural unities. World-history was the rise and flowering of national epochs. Organized society alone constituted history in this conception of the term. He called the collective social whole the national or popular spirit, the *Volksgeist.*

A people, said Hegel, is known by its deeds; it is what its deeds are.

It is a spirit having strictly defined characteristics, which erects itself into an objective world, that exists and persists in a particular religious form of worship, customs, constitution, and political laws—in the whole complex of its institutions—in the events and transactions that make up its history.[11]

To understand a people's spirit requires taking account of all their deeds. The *Volksgeist* represents the totality of "the spiritual powers that live in a people and rule it." These powers as they issue in various manifestations of a total social life he arranged in hierarchical ascent. On the first level he placed "physical needs", trades and technical arts, commercial and industrial life. Second came law and civil rights, family life, social divisions of class, government and the state. On the third level is religion, where the higher emotional life finds satisfaction in the Church. Finally, there are the sciences, natural, mathematical, artistic and philosophical. In them the intellectual demands of a national spirit are satisfied.[12] Hegel tried to see all these stages in their interrelatedness as the product of a single national spirit. The history of a people, he taught, is not a conglomeration of unrelated events. There is an essential connection, for instance, between Roman law and Roman religion, Roman literature and the Roman ethic.

The state, in the sense of the constitution and the organization of the government, occupied a central role in his understanding of the national spirit. It is the "basis and the middle point" of all concrete aspects of this many-sided life. In the political constitution, the governing structure of society, Hegel saw what made the nation or the people a universal, what bound the individual and the popular will into an organic unity. The state as the inner structure of a people was for him essentially the most concrete and the most rational aspect of the *Volksgeist*. For the constitution (conceived in its widest sense) extended throughout the total life of a nation. The organization of a people's life under a constitutional government was not held to be in opposition to other expressions of that life; rather it was that which best held the other forms together. In this sense the state signified for him a *Kulturstaat*.[13] The political was used as a wide category to include the most diverse spheres of social and institutional life.

A state is an individual totality, of which you cannot select any particular side, although a supremely important one, such as its political constitution; and deliberate and decide respecting it in that isolated form. Not only is that constitution most completely connected with and dependent on those other spiritual forces; but the form of the entire moral and intellectual individuality comprising all the forces it embodies, is only a step in the development of the grand whole—with its place preappointed in the process.[14]

After considering the whole course of civilization Hegel observed, "World-history is the history of states."

The ideal spheres in which national spirit objectifies its values Hegel conceived to be religion, fine arts and philosophy. In them he believed that a people attained to the clearest consciousness of principles and the substance of culture. Particularly in its religion he found the essential character of a nation's spirit. But here again it was religion understood in the widest sense, a sense peculiarly Hegelian. A revealing summary of his characterization of the nature of religion and its place in society occurs in the *Philosophy of History*.

Religion is the consciousness of a people of that which it is, of the existence of the highest. This knowledge is the universal essence. As a people represents God, so does it represent its relationship to God, or so does it represent itself. Thus religion is the concept a people has of its own nature.[15]

In another passage there is an even clearer exposition of the centrality of religion in the *Volksgeist*.

Religion is the sphere in which a nation gives itself the definition of that which it regards as the True. A definition contains everything that belongs to the essence of an object; reducing its nature to its simple characteristic predicate, as a mirror for every predicate—the generic soul pervading all its details. The conception of God, therefore, constitutes the general basis of a people's character.[16]

Within this wide interpretation of religion as consciousness of the substantial essence of cultural life, belong art and philosophy. Art, as unmediated concrete representation, portrays God in sensuous, external form, while philosophy, the consciousness of a nation's principles, portrays God in "freest and wisest form", with no need of a visible medium. Religion, in the more limited sense of faith and worship, adds to art devotion and reverence, producing the subjective feeling of community. Philosophy, through the medium of the concept, expresses and combines the subjective and objective aspects of religion and art, and conceives of the relation between individual and universal by means of thought. In these forms the spirit most fully realizes its freedom, and the *Volksgeist* becomes objectively aware of itself.

In portraying the development of the individual spirit, national culture and world history, Hegel made use of all the pageantry of his philosophical imagination. The experience of the individual is analogous to the experience of the nation, the experience of the nation to that of the human species as a whole. Cultures, like organisms, pass through the stages of growth, blossom, ripeness and decay. Like an individual they go through the periods of childhood, youth, adulthood, and senile decline. Nations, like individuals, eventually die a natural death. In their prime, they struggle to realize their purposes, to achieve in institutional form their inner potentialities.

> The highest point in the development of a people is this—to have gained a conception of its life and condition—to have reduced its laws, its ideas of justice and morality to a science; for in this unity (of the objective and subjective) lies the most intimate unity that spirit can attain to in and with itself.[17]

After a nation has achieved its purposes, the need for activity and struggle is gone. The spirit rests from its labors; like an old man it enjoys its past. It lives the life of custom—"custom is activity without opposition"—and such existence leads to natural death. A people does not actually cease to exist; but its historical importance is gone. Further life amounts to a kind of endless "vegetating", without intellect or vitality and with no universal significance.

With this organic conception of a nation's life, Hegel fused a dialectical consideration of the role of national spirit in history.[18] His organic analysis stressed the continuity and totality of national development, while his dialectical interpretation showed the inevitability of conflict and negation. Understood dialectically the history of a particular people is the movement between the poles of identity and contradiction, unity and conflict. The period of identity is the happy level when the individual is in harmony with the social whole. He finds his own happiness and fortune in following the common good. In such an epoch the citizens are moral, unified, vigorous. Forces of opposition, both within and without, are held in abeyance. The people actually achieve their grand objectives. They build the Athens of Pericles or the empire of the Caesars.

At the very peak of the nation's life, when the harmony of the individual and the social is most complete, appear the first intimations of decline and ruin. Even in this identity there is contradiction: spirit prepares its own ruin. The rise of reflective consciousness, the progress of individual education, bring about the destruction of the temporary equilibrium. Aggressive selfishness and private ambition replace service for the whole. The pain of internal conflict becomes acute. The real world becomes contrasted with the ideal. Individuals isolate themselves, flee into their private ideal world and live the life of the solitary. The people fall apart, lose their organic, vital unity and become disintegrated.

Paradoxically, it is in such periods of opposition and outward decline that national spirit attains its finest expression in ideal creations. As the end of a cultural cycle approaches, the spirit is ripe in wisdom. No longer able to express itself in public service, it turns within. The message of this ripened wisdom reveals a principle higher than the period of harmony had known. Contradiction has concealed a truth which now becomes evident and conscious. But this wisdom cannot save the people that produced it; indeed it is this very wisdom which contributes to their decline.

> The life of a people ripens a certain fruit; its activity aims at the complete manifestation of the principle which it embodies. But this fruit does not fall back into the bosom of the people that produced and matured it; on the contrary, it becomes a poison-draught to it. That poison-draught it cannot let alone, for it has an insatiable thirst for it; the taste of the draught is its annihilation, though at the same time the rise of a new principle.[19]

The rise of a new principle! The conflict of the real and the ideal, of the individual and his society, of selfish desire and universal law, that speeds the decline of a culture, has power also to result in a new synthesis. Another people, a new society, comes to life from the ashes of the old.

Pondering the record of the past with this faith in the dialectical progress of cultural principles, Hegel fused the infinitely varied record into a dramatic unity. Like Daniel's kingdoms, the history of mankind seemed to him to fall into four great epochs or cultural cycles—the first and fourth comprising many peoples and states, but unified by the same general principles. Unlike Daniel's, Hegel's four world epochs signified a continuous advance on the part of mankind. History had begun, not in a golden age, but in blind striving and "unconscious drives". Nature ruled over spirit. The control of reason was endlessly far from actualization in achieving human freedom. Natural necessities held undisputed sway. The spirit's light was obscured by manifestations of nature, both in the outer world and within the human being. But as spirit unfolded, the natural and instinctive were more and more controlled, suppressed and conquered. The power of thought was gradually becoming more dominant in history; the sway of the immediate and the purely natural was diminishing. Spirit advanced in levels or gradations, in each of which the self-awareness of freedom became more explicit.

The four kingdoms of this vision were the Oriental, Greek, Roman and Christian-Germanic.[20] In the ancient East the relation of spirit and nature had been an unequal union. Spirit was at one with nature in the sense that it was lost in nature at a sub-rational level within the human being. On the other hand, the Greek world found a harmonious and equal union, in which the natural was spiritualized and the spiritual was grounded in the natural. This unity was produced through immediate, artistic imagination. The Roman epoch witnessed an estrangement between spirit and nature, an unhappy dualism in which spirit had asserted its right in abstract independence of the natural, and the natural displayed its crushing force as a universal state power. Finally, the Christian world had arrived, according to Hegel, at a true reconciliation of the spiritual and natural by acknowledging the superiority of the reflective spirit and its consequent capacity to appropriate the natural for its own ends.

From the standpoint of modern criticism it is superfluous to say that this theory is not true in a literal or factual sense. It omits important periods and peoples, and oversimplifies the great diversity within the development of any people; creating, in the interests of a monistic logic, a single web of history that sometimes bears little relationship to actual events. Though Hegel's historical knowledge was vast, and though his clear-sighted grasp of the characteristic and essential is revealed in each of the cultural unities which he considered, we must agree that he did not do full justice to the empirical facts in the life of any people. But taken as a mythology, as a means of revealing Hegel's faith in the advance and progress of human ideals, this vision is not as fantastic and arbitrary as it has often been considered. We of the twentieth century cannot believe in the conception of progress as a unilinear path, or as a single pattern or structure. The idea of history as an unfolding process directed toward human freedom, and imperfectly but progressively realized by a few great historical peoples, seems both inadequate and unduly optimistic today. But it is the part of despair or of barren scepticism to believe that there is no advance, to see no pattern or patterns of development, no wisdom that is preserved in the rise and fall of peoples and their culture. To have no mythology and no vision is to disbelieve in the capabilities of human kind to achieve ideals.

Apart from its importance as vision, one of the consequences of Hegel's philosophy of history is that it brought onto the same plane all the manifestations of a nation's life and interpreted them on the basis of their interrelationships. The political and the artistic, the religious and the ethical, the legal and the philosophical, are all seen in the light of their temporal and social context. No single manifestation is exempt from dependence upon all other contemporary cultural factors; none can be properly understood when removed from the limitations of its time and place, or divorced from the spirit of the people from whom it arose. Hegel taught men to see that an understanding of the succession of principles and ideals which characterize social life and activity at a given time is possible only in the light of the full historical situation.[21]

According to this interpretation no principle, political, religious or ethical, is absolute or unconditioned; they are all relative, developing, subject to reformulation or replacement. Each cultural principle has fulfilled its destiny when it has served its time and satisfied the consciousness of the people from whom it sprang. Each cultural synthesis is absolute in its own time, each code of laws, each ethical persuasion, is truth for its age and people. But all must in the course of time give way to other codes and new persuasions; history knows no pause. This central conception of Hegel's vision of history has perhaps exercised the most profound influence on his own and on subsequent generations. This was an insight the implications of which had not been realized by the thinkers who preceded him. It has met with the general agreement of those who came after.

However, this phenomenology of spirit was not understood by Hegel as it was by certain of his followers in the sense of an endless succession of cultural principles without essential significance beyond their own time. Though he conceived the life of spirit to be in a sense organic, it is organic in a spiritual, rather than in a natural way. Though its products are relative and temporal, the actual life of the spirit is unending and absolute. For Hegel each cultural form possessed an eternal quality that did not pass away, but was retained and rendered ever present by reason of the activity of self-conscious thought. Hegel was in the habit of closing his introductory lectures on the *Philosophy of History* with this important emphasis on the place of the past in the present.

> While we are thus concerned exclusively with the idea of spirit, and in the history of the world regard everything as only its manifestation, we have in traversing the past . . . only to do with what is present; for philosophy, as occupying itself with the true, has to do with the eternally present. Nothing in the past is lost for it, for the idea is ever present. Spirit is immortal; with it there is no past, no future, but an essential *now*. . . . The life of the ever present spirit is a circle of progressive embodiments, which looked at in one aspect still exist beside each other, and only as looked at from another point of view appear as past. The grades which spirit seems to have left behind it, it still possesses in the depths of its present.[22]

These are a few of the leading motives of Hegel's philosophy of history. They will become more explicit in the following pages in which we shall be more concerned with the concrete interpretation of historical phenomena than with the logical structure and theory of history. In considering

Hegel's insights into the character of Greek culture, we shall see how they came from the knowledge, the interests and the problems of his own time. Before dealing with his mature thought, we should turn to his earliest interpretations of Hellenic civilization which grew out of his youthful studies.

II

YOUNG HEGEL'S DISCOVERY OF THE GREEKS

To understand young Hegel it is essential to realize the revolutionary character of his age. Seventeen hundred and seventy, the year in which he was born, has long been taken by historians as marking the beginning of a new era in Germany. Like a sleeper shaking off the bondage of recurring dreams, the country began to awaken to a new world. Its intellectual past had been mainly absorbed in a religious transcendentalism that had hardened into scholastic orthodoxy after the first great fervor of the Reformation epoch. The period immediately preceding 1770 brought across Germany's borders a new religion: the faith in worldly wisdom of the rationalists of the Enlightenment, a religion which condemned all dogmas except the dogma of the self-sufficiency of human reason. This penetration of the Enlightenment from without brought a stream of intellectual influences that transformed Germany and for a time seemed likely to alienate her people from the past and from their own as yet unproved genius.

But the epoch in which Hegel came to maturity saw a double reaction. The youth of Germany were in revolt. They scorned, on the one hand, the rationalistic wisdom of the Enlightenment, and on the other, the acceptance of the world as a place in which to perfect humility. Where these two movements of rationalism and religious orthodoxy had become allied, as was the case in many of the schools, their revolt was doubly bitter. In flight from the imported worldly doctrines of the Enlightenment and the religious heritage of medieval theology now grown inflexible, they sought a new basis of faith, a new mythology, a new vision. In the ferment of those years, they looked abroad for guidance, abroad and to the past. And among the many cross currents they found a compelling ideal in the ancient Hellenic culture. Often accepted uncritically, and among the more romantic enthusiasts freely compounded with other and foreign elements, this neo-Hellenism or neoclassicism became for a time the dominant force in German intellectual life. And because many of these leaders were gifted beyond measure, they succeeded to a remarkable degree in loosening Germany from her traditional moorings, and giving her a new humanistic and ideal orientation that was to influence the whole of Western civilization.

The story is long and complicated, and it is no part of my purpose to continue with generalizations on the period as a whole. It suffices to recognize that the course of young Hegel's development was not an uncommon one. He was drawn into the current of his time, and while he differed from the others in his conclusions, he was at one with them in his aspirations. They all dreamed of a coming age when humanity would be elevated to a new level of attainment, when man would emancipate himself from his old bondage to dogmas and selfishness. They sought for a new relationship of man to the divine, which would permit him to go with upright head and a joyous heart, not forgetting piety, but with a piety born of confidence that man is something in his own right, that he shares in God's work. In this sense all the writers from Lessing and Herder to Schelling and Hegel were marshalled under one standard, that of the ideally human. And herein lies the significance of Nietzsche's dictum that the Germans "belong to the day before yesterday and the day after tomorrow—they have had as yet no today". The men of Hegel's generation were striving for a today, but were living for a tomorrow and drawing much of the inspiration for their vision of the future from yesterday. A large part of this yesterday was the Hellenism which, having gathered impetus from the initial work of Winckelmann and Herder, was perpetuated and idealized in the writings of Goethe and Schiller, and reached its apotheosis in Schelling, Hölderlin and Hegel.

From his boyhood Hegel's thoughts reflect the varying and powerful currents of the time. Karl Rosenkranz, the author of the first significant biography, has preserved some of the early entries in a journal that seems to have been begun by Hegel at the age of eight and continued in a desultory manner throughout his life. Much of it is in Latin, and includes lengthy excerpts from his reading, a practice for which Hegel is famous. No one can read these early entries without realizing the enthusiasm of this youth for learning of all kinds, an enthusiasm that drove him to spend much of his allowance for books. From the first he showed an unusual interest in knowledge of the cultural-historical kind. He was prompted to study civilizations rather than individuals, periods of history, social trends, the large general sweep rather than striking single events or individual men. And everywhere his eye was for facts, bare historical facts and more facts; they were his passion. That is perhaps the only striking trait in the picture we possess, a picture otherwise typical enough of many intelligent, thorough, gymnasial students—a picture not, however, so colorless and mediocre as many biographers have painted it.

Among the fragments of his essays written during the years at the Stuttgart gymnasium, and also published by Rosenkranz, two are of some importance and deserve brief attention. The first, written in August 1787 at the age of seventeen, is entitled "Concerning the Religion of the Greeks and Romans". The second, on "Some Characteristic Differences of the Ancient Poets", of which only a part has been printed, was written a year later. In condemnation of the superstitions and idolatries of popular religion, the first of these essays illustrates the true spirit of eighteenth century rationalism. The contrast with Hegel's later work on folk-religion is complete, and for that reason the little essay of five closely written pages is interesting. Young Hegel supposes that the path which Greece and Rome followed in their religion is the way that all peoples go. From an early superstitious worship of an all-powerful, fearful and capricious divinity, they created pantheons and sacred groves where they sought help in times of trouble and prepared costly sacrifices to win favors and gain knowledge of the future. The priests, "the more clever and crafty" among the people, helped to inculcate the superstition through a multiplicity of ceremonies. But the wise men of Greece, the truly "enlightened", were soon to develop more worthy concepts of divinity, to make a union of morality and good deeds with happiness. At this point the "religion of reason" began its development and pressed to its goal through many paths of error. The youth concludes that these manifold errors should convince everyone of the difficulty of arriving at truth, and should induce us to inspect our "inherited and propagated opinions, even those which it has never occurred to us to question, to see if they can be considered perhaps false or half-true".[1] There is in this rather typical product of the Enlighten-ment as yet hardly a hint of the direction the young university student is to take and painstakingly pursue.

But the case is different with the second and more often mentioned of these adolescent essays, that "Concerning Characteristic Differences of the Old Poets". The contrast is between ancient and modern poets and not as the title might imply among the ancients themselves. Poets of the modern day, wrote Hegel, do not enjoy the influence the old poets had for several reasons. The moderns deal with historical deeds and legends but they procure the material out of books, not from the oral tradition. Much of the folklore too is taken from foreign peoples, and has no essential relation to the religion or true history of the German people. Consequently, the interest has largely shifted from content to the art of the poet. The ancients, on the other hand, possessèd a striking "simplicity" which con-sisted in faithful portrayal of a single historical occurrence, without obscure allusions or personal idiosyncrasies. Their works elaborated stories with which their hearers were already fully acquainted. The classical writers[2] were original, that is, they were not dependent on books for their knowledge, this "cold book-learning which imprints its dead symbols

on the brain". Their ideas came straight from experience, and in spite of
all they knew they could still tell "How? Where? Why? they learned it!"[3]

Moreover, the classical poets wrote "without consideration for their
public", following the course of their own ideas uninhibited. But today
dramatists know that their works will be read, and they write for a reading
public as well as an audience. And so on. Here is the temper of the coming
Hegel, the sense of contrasting cultures, the emphasis on the natural and
uninhibited, a tendency to set up the ancient as the standard by which to
measure the modern. As an eighteen-year-old student he already possessed
the sense for large objective values and cultural traits that was to characterize his later work.

It is in this spirit and with these interests that Hegel pursued his further
education at Tübingen, where the companionship of Hölderlin and the
younger Schelling did more to confirm than to moderate his esteem for the
ancients. The story of the three in the Tübingen seminary has often been
told. The time was one of great excitement in the outside world because
of the French Revolution. Like nearly all of intellectual Germany, these
three greeted it as the dawn of a new day and eagerly proclaimed its watchwords. But for all the excitement and stir, these events were foreign and
far away, and their influence, though powerful, was channeled into the
more immediate reactions which the youths experienced from the theological, literary and philosophical studies in their own small school. The world
stored in books was the world they felt most intimately. Though French
authors, particularly Rousseau, were read assiduously, one cannot escape
the impression that Hegel and his friends were not very closely touched by
the spirit of political and social revolt so rampant in that day. They were
rebels, true enough—but in the intellectual realm and against intellectual
tyranny. Their passionate concern was to gain a new religious and an
aesthetic philosophy. They worshipped, above all, the vital and the joyful,
the qualities they felt most lacking in German educational and intellectual life.

And in these years it was Schiller—as Theodor Haering's recent book
entitled *Hegel: sein Wollen und sein Werk* particularly shows—who was
their hero. More especially, it was the Schiller of the philosophical poems,
the Schiller who had drunk of Grecian wine, and who longed for unity of
life in a beautiful naturalism, such as the Greeks of his imagination
enjoyed. The first form of his famous poem, "Die Götter Griechenlands",
with its lament for the lost joys of pagan life contrasted with the gloom of
modern Christian existence, found nowhere more responsive hearers than
in the "communism of spirits" at Tübingen. His "Lied an die Freude" was
equally important. These songs and fiery dramas determined for them the

liberating code: *Life, Freedom, Love,* and the Greek formula *hen kai pan,* that included all three in the all-one, became the mystic symbol of their friendship. This was their answer, as young men first coming into the possession of their powers, to orthodox Lutheran theology and the rationalistic dualisms of a day which they felt to be passing. Some time later Hegel wrote to his friend Hölderlin in the verse of the poem, "Eleusis", reminding him of the old schoolboy resolves, "of the pact, which no oath sealed, to live only for free truth, and never, never to come to terms with the statute which rules opinion and feeling".[4] The friends were soon to part, each to go his own way, and unhappily to forfeit the intimate understanding of their youth. But each in his own fashion carried the ideals there conceived forward along new paths.

Hegel spent the eight years after Tübingen as *Hauslehrer* in Bern and Frankfurt. They were obscure, perhaps unhappy, years, and it was long believed that they were unproductive. Hegel was slow in coming to maturity. Even when he was appointed as lecturer to the University of Jena in 1800 he gave little promise of a successful career. Not until 1806 did his first important work appear, and then it seems to have come as a considerable surprise to many who knew him intimately. But scholars of the twentieth century realize that the decade after Tübingen was not lacking in growth and creative output. The *Phenomenology of Spirit* did not spring from a mind that was immature or inexperienced in intellectual discovery. It was germinating throughout these years and for this reason Hegel's twenties and early thirties have become a source of fruitful enquiry for students of philosophy.

Wilhelm Dilthey may be said to have begun the research on young Hegel. He first made a careful study of the difficult holographs preserved in the *Königliche Bibliothek* in Berlin. Dilthey was interested in arriving at an historical understanding of Hegel's philosophical development and his short but valuable study, *Die Jugendgeschichte Hegels,* is deservedly ranked with the best that he has written. A year later his student and close friend, Hermann Nohl, published, under the title of *Hegels theologische Jugendschriften,* the manuscripts from which Dilthey had drawn. This proved to be an extensive collection of some 400 pages of manuscript, carefully edited and entitled. Many of the texts are incomplete, without introductions and with interruptions in the middle of sentences, or more often whole pages are lacking here and there in an essay.

This publication with Dilthey's fine commentary has awakened an entirely new interest in Hegel, and the past thirty years have seen an increasing number of critical works on the genesis and development of his ideas. Franz Rosenzweig[5] first attempted a genetic study of the philosopher's political ideas. More recently, Theodor Haering has written a large, two-volume biographical analysis of which the first volume, of nearly 800 pages, is a minute account of Hegel's early years. Other less ambitious works have also appeared or are in preparation. Hegel is now receiving the kind of scholarly attention long given to the study of Kant.

But a certain type of emphasis upon these youthful essays may be carried to an extreme. It is hard to sympathize with the word-by-word analysis of Haering. It is also misleading to find in these fragments, as Kuno Fischer has professed to do, all the main currents of Hegel's mature system. They do not form a harmonious whole nor can they stand alone as an independent portrayal of a philosophical position. Too often scholars have passed over contradictions and incompatible ideas, sometimes with a word of recognition, sometimes without. It seems obvious to me that Hegel was here seeking a point of view, that he was trying to become clear in his own mind as to what he believed, rather than expressing his thought for others. Later he was to change many of these early opinions, to develop many that are only hinted at in these writings, and to lose interest in at least some of the problems that then concerned him. It ought to be significant that he never showed any intention of publishing or completing these early efforts; he did not even preserve a clean copy. He lifted out certain portions for use in lectures, revised them at will, and made no attempt to keep them intact. They should be regarded as a record of Hegel's struggle to arrive at a consistent and valid understanding of the problems that vexed him, as a diary of his development, private, careless, unsystematic, incomplete. As such they are valuable and interesting. Dilthey declared that Hegel wrote "nothing more beautiful", and there is truth in his judgment. For they do contain passages which are fresh and spontaneous to a degree that is hard to find in the work of the older man. Hegel's genius for historical insight and cultural criticism was at its best before the logical system and the "pageantry of his metaphysics" had weighted down his thought. Though the works appear immature in the tendency to overstate, and suffer from an almost idolatrous reverence for Hellenic civilization, they gain all the more in boldness of statement, in wealth of ideas and in warmth of conception and expression.[6]

It should be noted at the outset that almost all these writings are concerned with religious problems. Nohl has appropriately entitled them *Hegels theologische Jugendschriften*. They deal mainly with problems that concerned the aged Kant and led to his *Religion innerhalb der Grenzen der blossen Vernunft*. In addition to reflecting the intellectual atmosphere of the time, they suggest Hegel's religious background and early training from which he had already reacted, and suggest the focus of interest that was to remain in some degree central throughout his life. Certain of them, notably the essay on *Das Leben Jesu*, show little difference in point of view from the general attitude of the Enlightenment on Christian history. The moral justification of religion is here opposed to dogma, ritual and theology. Young Hegel is obviously acquainted with earlier critiques of religion by such men as Mendelssohn, Lessing, Shaftesbury and, particularly, Kant. It is easy to detect the general influence of the rationalists but not nearly so easy to determine on which points he differs from them and at whom his polemics are directed.

The relation to Kant is a particularly vexed question. Dilthey believed that the two were in fairly consistent agreement on fundamentals, but the fragments do not on the whole appear to support his opinion. In general, it may be said that Hegel's quarrel was not with Kant's affirmation of the primacy of the ethical sphere in religion. His opposition, now and later, was to the Kantian dualisms of reason and sense, and of duty and desire. Hegel inclined toward reconciliation and unity of life in individuals and peoples, and his sharp, often bitter attacks on Kant in these early documents were directed against the sundering process which destroyed what is vital, joyful and productive in religion and in life.

Such is the theme of the fragments included under the title of *Volksreligion und Christentum*. They are pervaded with a sense of the deep meaning of religion for a vital social consciousness. A true folk-religion serves the people, expressing and conserving their best values and at the same time satisfying their aspirations. For a people's life is grounded and sustained, said Hegel, in the senses, in feeling and in imagination, and religion must be similarly grounded if it is to have vitality and power. All his natural vehemence is applied to the attack upon the rationalists' belief in a religion purged of superstition and myth. Real religion is of the heart; its ideal is a "subjectivity" which renders superfluous any form of dogmatic or positivistic creeds. On the other hand, Hegel contrasts folk-religion with *Privatreligion*, the purpose of which is "to cultivate the morality of isolated individuals". *Volksreligion* is by its very nature a public phenomenon which cannot even be thought of apart from other phases of a people's life. It permeates the manifold spheres of their interests, determining political and moral, private and sensuous motives and actions. The spirit of the people, its history, religion, the degree of its political freedom—none of these can be really understood in isolation. They are all united, says Hegel, like three colleagues so united that no one of them can act alone but each always limits the others.

The simile suggests a deep-seated conviction which was to remain throughout his later life. At this early stage religion for him meant the path to enjoyment and unhindered participation of the whole individual in the comprehensive needs of life. Later it came to mean more, but the emphasis on this central function persisted. His humanistic insistence on the importance of imagination, vitality and joy kept them as the chief categories to be desired in religion.

> When gladness and joy must be abashed before religion, when he who has made merry at a public festival must steal back into the temple, then the form of religion presents too gloomy an exterior, to expect that for the sake of its demands one should renounce the pleasures of life.[7]

It is evident that Hegel's ideal religion was not a figment of his imagination, that his gaze was fixed on one concrete example. Again and again in this treatise and in all the related fragments it is Greek religion that stands out in glowing contrast to Judaism, the early Christian church and modern Christianity. One need only listen to the words of the hymn to the Greeks, found in the early pages of Nohl's collection, to realize how completely Hegel's concept of folk-religion is permeated by Hellenic paganism.

> Alas, from the distant days of the past an image comes before a soul possessing a feeling for human beauty, for the greatness in the great. It is the image of a people of genius among nations, a son of fortune, of freedom, an elect of fair fancy. He too was chained to mother earth by the iron bond of necessity, but by the aid of his feelings and imagination he so elaborated it, so refined and beautified it, and with the aid of the graces so entwined it with roses, that he was satisfied with these fetters, as if they were his own work, a part of himself. His servants were gladness, joy, and grace; the consciousness of their power and their freedom filled his soul. His more serious playmates were friendship and love, not the faun, but sensitive-souled Amor, adorned with all the graces of heart and lovely dreams.[8]

The power of this pagan vision becomes more fully apparent when Hegel opposes it to the Christendom of his day. How easily he had shaken off all supernaturalism and taken a wholly humanistic, not to say naturalistic, position! Later he was to adopt a more appreciative attitude toward the established religion of his own civilization, but in this period he condemned it in sweeping terms.

That judgment, though present in most of the fragments, is most forcefully stated in a longer essay entitled *Positivität der christlichen Religion*. Every people, declares Hegel, has its own objects of imagination and feeling, its gods, angels, devils or saints, that live through the generations in popular tradition. Free peoples all possess some sort of factual history of old heroes who won them their freedom, founded the state, or freed them from pressing danger. Through "national imagination" such exploits find expression in public festivals to honor the god or hero, or in sacred shrines to which the people turn as the object of their adoration. Even if some of their national symbols were borrowed, as was the case of the Egyptians, Greeks and Romans, still they became largely assimilated and made conformable to daily life and ideals. Religion in these lands served to unify and preserve popular tradition.

That primary function is what Hegel tried to emphasize, and it was just here that he believed Christianity had miserably failed. It had not become incorporated in the imagination or in the living ideals of the peoples who adopted it. Instead of garnering the products of their history, it had warred against them. Germans, Gauls and Scandinavians had lost their gods, their heroes, their legends. "Christianity depopulated Valhalla and destroyed the sacred groves," branding as base superstition the living national myths. Instead of a cultus drawn from their own past, this religion of the Orient transferred to the German people legends of a race whose climate, laws and persuasions were completely alien. Instead of a Charlemagne or a Friedrich Barbarossa, we are given, says this young German, a David and a Solomon.

These pages are embittered with invective. What of the wars that devoured millions of Germans, the battles fought to win basic rights for the German people, and now at the end their descendants cannot say why or wherefore! At cost of their life-blood, our forefathers attained by the Reformation the right to follow their own religious destiny and how is it remembered? By the occasional reading in church of the Augsburg Confession which bores the hearers. So has that which is our own and which should form the living substance of our popular religious faith given place to the purposes of Christianity. In these words there rings a consciousness of the lasting incompatibility between the religion of an ancient and world-weary wisdom and the exuberance of a young and unsatiated experience.

How different the case had been in Greece! "He who, unacquainted with the history, the culture, the legislation of the city of Athens, lived within her walls but one year, could learn to know them fairly well by observing the festivals."[9] For there the Athenian citizen, even if his poverty deprived him of the city's rights and forced him to become a slave, knew as well as did Pericles or Alcibiades, who Agamemnon was or Oedipus. He could enjoy with the richest the deeds of heroes immortalized by the poets in public verse and by the sculptors in marble.

More than this, Greek popular religion had what Hegel held to be most necessary for the vitality of religious and national imagination. It singled out certain definite spots where sacred history had been enacted. Religious imagination needs a living presence, a physical and spiritual nearness. With this emphasis Hegel explained the special importance of the autochthonous divinities of Greece. In the same connection, he explained and approved the warm faith of Catholics in their saints, particularly in those who wrought miracles in their own localities. For such works of grace the people have an intimate feeling that they do not derive from the more universal miracles of Christ himself.

Again and again Hegel returns to this theme in different forms, always emphasizing what is essentially foreign in Christian mythology in contrast with the homogeneity and warmth of the religious faith of the Greeks. It is evident, however, that more than actual religion is in his mind; he is also considering the part religion plays in uniting a people politically and socially. National imagination (Nationalphantasie), about which he likes to speak, obviously means more to him than a sacred cult. Naturally and without much explanation he here treats the sacred and secular together; he was later to emphasize how unwarranted is their separation. Dwelling on German folk-lore and history, he envisaged, if only vaguely, a German state in which union might grow out of the sense of a common past. The ideal would be a union of church and state, with religion as the cohesive bond, indeed the very soul. Dilthey points out that for this the Greek city-state was Hegel's obvious guide, but his eye was also on the future though what he saw there was as yet neither clear nor hopeful.

It cannot be claimed that these essays contain much revolutionary fervor for a new society. A strain of sadness and a sense of futility pervade them. From the old Teutonic lore young Hegel returns to the sober conclusion that it is useless, worse than useless, to attempt to revive this past, for it is stranger and more foreign to the modern German "than the Ossianic or the Indian". But the pessimistic conviction that understanding this better past cannot lead to its renewal did not lessen his ardor for contrasting Greek antiquity with the life of the present. From comparing the religious outlook of the Greeks with his own Christian culture, Hegel turned to the consideration of the ethical and political consequences. The festivals of the Greeks, even the bacchanals, were all religious festivals. They honored a god or hero who had done service for the state. When a Greek enjoyed unusual success in any sphere, he made a festival to the god whose favor had made it possible. Hegel cites Agathon in Plato's *Symposium*. These were occasions of joy and celebration, here was joyous homage paid by man to the divine. Again the young rebel draws a painful contrast with Christian worship. Christianity seeks to make men "citizens of heaven", and with eyes fixed on the sky completely loses sight of all "human sentiments". It passes over the natural connection of religion and conduct, and destroys the necessary union of the human and divine. The Christian sacrament is placed beside the Grecian sacrifice to emphasize the modern failure to achieve this unity.

> At our greatest public festival one approaches the celebration of the sacred gift in the clothes of mourning and with lowered eyes. At the festival which should be the celebration of universal brotherhood, many a one feels that he may become infected by the brotherly cup from which one diseased drank before him. And in order that one's spirit may not be attentive, not maintained in its sacred emotion, one must get the offering out of one's pocket and place it on the plate during the celebration. In contrast, the Greeks approached the altars of their gods, laden with the friendly gifts of nature, crowned with garlands of flowers, garbed in colors of gladness, their open countenances inviting to friendship and love and disseminating cheer.[10]

Hegel's judgment is harsher still when he confronts the Christian view of Providence with the Greek conception of Fate. In his mature system these important beliefs were to receive very different treatment, and the Christian was acknowledged to be a great advance upon the Greek. But here neither is analyzed very far, and the colors are black and white. He says in effect that a divine and beneficent Providence is the Christian's answer to all the misfortunes of life. Christianity bids man suffer in silence, firm in the conviction that all is for the best, and that misfortunes are to be understood as punishment for one's own or one's ancestors' sin. His solace is the command to pray without ceasing, and to look to the world to come for the righting of wrong. The greater the suffering, the more glorious will be the joy in that day. But when the Christian revolts, nothing is more common than to see him presuming to be master of his fate and director of his own paths. Men who do this, writes Hegel, adopt the heroic ideas of an idealistic philosophy and lose all vestiges of human piety.

The Greeks avoided these extremes. Their faith was built on the secure foundation of "natural necessity". They recognized that the gods favored the good and punished the evil-doer with a fearful Nemesis, but they were not misled by the pitiful desire to see everything as best. "Misfortune to them was misfortune, misery was misery, what had happened and could not be changed, they were not disposed to brood about, for their *moira*, their *ananke tyche* was blind."[11] Because they were accustomed to recognize necessity, it was possible for them to submit with resignation. And Hegel concludes that this faith of the Greeks, since it possesses respect for natural necessity on the one hand, and on the other carries the conviction that men are ruled by the gods according to moral laws, seems to be humanly conformable to the sublimity of the divine and the weakness of man, his dependence upon nature and his limited vision.[12]

But when he goes on from the appraisal of modern Christianity and ancient Greece to an evaluation of Judaism, Hegel uses a different measuring rod. Here his criterion is the degree of harmony with the natural order attained by the Greek and the Hebrew civilizations. In his short sketch of Jewish history, drawn from the Bible and Josephus, Hegel's condemnation is as complete as it was of modern Christendom. On almost every page of the essay *Der Geist des Judentums* he sets side by side comparable events of Greek and Jewish history. If we should automatically adopt the categories opposite to those with which he judges the Jews, we should arrive at his estimation of the Greek.

He finds Judaism, a religion *aus Unglück und fürs Unglück*, in a special sense epitomized in Abraham whose experience typified the fate of succeeding generations. Abraham left his home-land without apparent cause to become a wanderer and stranger, without a state, without definite ties to any social group. His own existence was his most important treasure. Separation and opposition were the significant elements in his life. He could win no relationship to the land in which he lived. Nature was his enemy. Against this picture of the friendless wanderer, young Hegel poses Kadmus and Danaus who also left their fatherland, but not without a struggle; "they sought a country where they might be free to love the soil. Abraham could not love the land and therefore he could not be free."[13]

Out of this enmity with earth and peoples were formed, in Hegel's view, the religious and moral concepts of Judaism. Abraham, the exposed stranger, "needed a ruler, a helper", above and beyond, by whose power he could escape physical and spiritual want. His religion was a "religion of need". Dependence found its comfort in the all-powerful deity. Abraham's God was as foreign to other peoples and as full of enmity as was Abraham himself. The very root of his godhead, as young Hegel saw it, was hatred; his sole care was for his chosen ones. In this he was unlike the gods of Greece and Rome who benefited their own particular people, to be sure, but who never presumed to look with despite on other nations' gods.

This dependence on an absolute god which arose as a consequence of the dualism of nature and man, Hegel used to interpret the Jewish civil government and to contrast it with the laws of Greece. Jewish legislation, he insisted, sprang from the thought of God as master, and of man as significant only in relationship to Him. The Mosaic laws of property are compared with those of Solon and Lycurgus on the restriction of inequalities of wealth. Though outwardly similar, they originate in a completely different conception of life. In the Greek republics the laws were aimed at preventing loss of freedom by impoverished citizens and a consequent lack of participation on their part in political activity. Among the Jews, who really possessed no rights or property but simply held all in trust as borrowed, equality meant lack of citizenship. Hegel compresses his comment into one harsh aphorism: "The Greek laws provided for equality, because the Greeks were free and independent; the Mosaic laws provided equality among the Jews, because all of them lacked capacity for independence."[14]

Hegel was also conscious of the sharp antithesis between pagan polytheism and Jewish monotheism. But he had not yet found the explanation for it which he was later to give in his lectures on the *Philosophy of Religion*. At the present point he is only certain that the Greek gods came into being out of a sense of oneness with nature, that they were not really rulers, but fellow creatures of beauty and play. The gods of Greece were not supreme; man maintained his dignity and worth. The Greek divinities sprang from a beauty which itself overcame the fundamental dualism that conquered the Jewish world. This is the recurring emphasis of Hegel's treatment of Jewish history. He sums it all up in one harsh closing paragraph:

> The great tragedy of the Jewish people is no Greek tragedy. It can awaken neither pity nor fear, for both arise only from the fate of a necessary transgression of a beautiful being. That of the Jews can but arouse abhorrence. The fate of the Jewish people is the fate of Macbeth, who abandoned the path of nature, clung fast to foreign beings, and in their service was forced to crush and murder everything sacred in human nature. Deserted finally by his gods . . . he was annihilated by his very faith.[15]

The value of this contrast for the present purpose lies in the light it throws on Hegel's Hellenic ideal; it should not be considered as his final judgment of the Hebrew spirit. More than once he was to alter his early conception in the years of his maturity. As Karl Rosenkranz pointed out, Jewish culture and its role in history remained for Hegel a vexing problem throughout his life. He could not come to a clear and definite judgment upon it, but later he found positive value in some of the qualities which at this time appeared to him to be negative. The *Philosophy of History* ranked Jewish monotheism with its conception of justice higher in the sphere of consciousness than Greek polytheism and necessity.

The contrast between early Christianity and Hellenism remains to be considered. Just here in the relation of the message of the gospels to the best qualities of paganism young Hegel shows the acuteness of his insight in weighing essential characteristics of the declining pagan and ascending Christian ways of life. His judgments here are less harsh and absolute, though his sympathy is still overwhelmingly on the side of humanistic religion. But when he considers Christ as a person and evaluates his teaching Hegel's future synthesis between the classic and the Christian can be foreseen. In his pages on love and reconciliation, forgiveness and the conquest of law by grace, there are traces of the mystical, romantic spirit that has often been spoken of in these fragments. But the main drive is unquestionably away from the subjectivity and irrationalism of mysticism. He was struggling to understand the personal and individual values which Jesus embodied, to do them justice and to see the necessity of their triumph over the pagan world. But the stumbling block by which he was repelled was the strictly private nature of Jesus' ideal.

So we are drawn back to the distinction between a living folk-religion and a private personal faith. In Jesus' advice to the rich young ruler Hegel saw what was for him decisive: a training in individual perfection only, with no concern for society. Later he realized the necessity for Christianity to develop from the faith of a few individuals into a world-religion and when he had reached this[16] point he could attribute to Jesus the highest subjective value. He now believed it was due to special historical circumstances that the earliest Christianity had become a sectarian creed. In a long historical sketch, also included among these early papers, Hegel paints an unlovely picture of the Jewish world when Christ appeared. Disunity and factionalism, which even the common hatred of a Roman oppressor could not resolve, were outer manifestations of inner tragedy. Against this background Jesus came in complete opposition to the spirit of his time and people. He sought no freedom from foreign bondage, but reconciliation with themselves through the doctrine of love. As Hegel sets the morality of love against the Hebrew concept of justice, the inner intention against the outer act, reconciliation against punishment, it is plain that for him the tragedy of Jesus lay not in his own teaching but in the people whom he taught. The inevitability of his rejection lay in their dependence on an absolute deity and their slavery to law.

Nevertheless, there was for Hegel the strongest contrast with Greek life in the fact that Jesus' teachings were for the individual alone. One of the most interesting sections in the fragments concerns Socrates and Jesus as teachers and educators. To the few enthusiasts whose ears were not stopped, Jesus became a personified ideal. They worshipped him as master and lord; already accustomed to dependence and dictation, they submitted their lives and characters to him. They kept and guarded his words, as initiates of his truth. He was the master, they his subjects. How different was the case with Socrates! To quote Hegel's words, he was a republican among republicans, an equal who sought to be no more than an equal. With "fine urbanity", which Hegel delights to dwell upon, he approached all sorts of men, joined in their talk with a freedom that permitted even a slave to maintain his point of view. In simple, incidental ways he led up to topics that concerned their highest good. At no time was there any show of dictation, no assertion that Socrates had the truth and was simply telling it. His was no preaching from chancel or even mountainside. "How could it ever have occurred to a Socrates in Greece to preach?" He gave no occasion for any one to say, "Is this not the son of Sophroniscus? Whence came his wisdom that he should try to teach us?" Instead, Socrates remained an object of laughter among his fellow Greeks.

The irony in the implied contrast with Jesus grows sharper as young Hegel proceeds. Instead of a selected group, Socrates had followers of all sorts—"or rather none at all". His friends were numerous, but in no sense was he their head or lord. He had no wish to mold them to a single type; he wanted no inner circle who knew the watchwords, wore the same garb and were of one mind. His student comrades came from every walk of life, and they remained in their accustomed callings. They were not "heroes in martyrdom and suffering, but in deeds and living". Like Socrates, his friends retained the responsibilities of social life; they were not apart from, but a part of Greek life.

Why did the pagan philosophy fall a victim to the Christian faith? Why does the Occident live under the Christian rather than the pagan emblem? How could an ancient, indigenous religion, firmly established in the state, responsible in the minds of the people for the origins of cities and constitutions,—a religion beneath whose banners armies fought and believed themselves protected, a religion in whose service all festivals were arranged,—how could such a belief have been supplanted by a foreign cult? Hegel, like others of his generation, thought these questions important, and struggled to find their answer. The conventional reply of pious Christians that when Christianity came the people saw the folly of their myths and recognized the all-sufficiency of the new faith was obviously inadequate. The adherents of the pagan faith, says Hegel, "are still so superior to us in everything that is great, beautiful, noble, and free that we can only marvel at these beings as a generation wholly strange to us."[17]

No, the answer is not to be found in the character of the two religions but in the "spirit of the age". "A quiet, secret revolution" unexampled elsewhere in history, must necessarily have preceded the transition. The religion of Greece and Rome had been a religion of and for democratic peoples. Men followed laws they had themselves enacted. They were fettered by no abstract morality since the state and social usage determined what was right.

But successful wars and the increase of riches and luxury in Athens and Rome gradually gave superiority to a few, who asserted their supremacy by force. The individual began to dominate the social; democratic equality and independence disappeared; the idea of freedom as self-determination was gone. Hegel here expresses in two compact sentences what he was to elaborate in later years:

> The image of the state as a product of his own activity disappeared from the soul of the citizen; the care and the supervision of the whole rested in the soul of a single individual, or of a few. . . . The freedom to obey self-imposed laws, to follow self-elected governments in peace and commanders in war, to carry out plans resolved upon in common accord with others, disappeared; all political freedom was suppressed; the right of the citizen was now only the claim to the security of property which henceforth filled his whole world.[18]

The citizen had lost his sense of belonging to a state and of living for an idea. His own life and his own property were all in all to him, and death became a terror. In the great age the republic lived on though the citizen died, but now nothing that man cared for survived him. The free republican who fought and died for his state asked no recompense except to win renown among the living and in death to consort with the brave. But now, having lost the objective content of life, the unattached individual could no longer face death with equanimity; hence arose his longing for the soul to be "something eternal".

The old gods no longer sufficed; they could not sustain the "individual". His fathers had been content with gods who showed all the frailty of men, "for every man had the eternal and the self-sufficient within his own breast".[19] As Schiller had written, the gods were more human then, but the men were more divine. That was Hegel's conviction too. With loss of independence and reliance on human power, came the need for an absolute, omnipotent godhead to whom alone goodness and freedom could be attributed. Subjective religion became objective, the religion of imagination gave way to positive faith. This new religion depended on a person as the object of wonder and veneration and was characterized by signs and miracles which gave assurance that individual life survived death. A powerless posterity fled to the altar, offering up their persons and the present for the sake of a future and a beyond. They renounced all interest in society, were content with the basest despotism and slavery, exulted in their misery on earth that they might gain happiness in heaven.

Young Hegel goes on to trace from this "spirit of the time" the rise of basic Christian dogmas such as the doctrine of original sin and the depravity of man. He does not scruple to label it "slavery and depravity". One could easily imagine these to be pages from Feuerbach or Nietzsche. Here speaks the voice of the complete humanist for whom the loss of freedom meant incapacity for independence. In the midst of his historical analysis the contemporary problem keeps asserting itself. Again and again comes the cry for a more *menschenfreundliche* religion, to transform Christian civilization into something closer to the humanist ideal. In one striking sentence Hegel utters his belief that his own age could push away, at least "in theory", from the negative character of Christian culture.

> Aside from earlier attempts it has been reserved for our day especially, to lay claim to the treasures which were formerly squandered on heaven, to lay claim to them as the property of man, at least in theory; but which age will have the strength to make this claim valid and to gain possession of them wholly?[20]

This is young Hegel's dominant ideal. In his own way he was as revolutionary as any of his generation. He had drunk as deeply as the others of the wine of the French Revolution, and he was, more than most, a fugitive from the immediate past. Recognizing this, we must remember that we have here considered only the formulations of his *Jugendschriften*. The opinions expressed in them are neither complete nor final, but they indicate the way his thought was tending; they set problems, and offer suggestions which reappear in the work of the mature philosopher. In addition to the need for complete spiritual reorientation, they reveal, though still in a half-conscious form, the urgent longing for some kind of national unity and thoroughgoing political and social reform. Two short political treatises which Hegel published during these years, one on the Constitution of Württemberg, the other on the Constitution of Germany, give specific and realistic expression to this desire. To transform the Germany of his own day which was merely a *Gedankenstaat* into a reality powerful enough to unify the petty German states, Hegel called for a modern Theseus.

But the emphasis on a *Volksreligion* is the element in the early writings that is most significant for Hegel's future. In it he saw the means for achieving and maintaining national unity. As is the religion of a people, so in large measure will be its government, ethics, art and philosophy. This was the emphasis which he was later to repeat. It was the unifying power of the pagan religion that fastened his attention on Hellenism. Popular religion conceived as kinship with one's antecedents, one's people, and with the natural universe was the ideal that, despite his rationalistic temperament, became in Hegel an almost mystical force. In "Eleusis", the poem already mentioned which he wrote to Hölderlin at the age of twenty-six, this vision of a folk-religion as the only lasting and true faith is suffused with prophetic fervor. It describes the mystery cult, whose "public secrets" Hegel saw embodied in the ethical order and traditions of the Greeks.

He imagines himself walking in the cool of the evening; stillness reigns about him and within. In imagination he is carried back to the secret shrine where Ceres is enthroned. The wisdom of her priests has long been silent; no searching can recover a word or a sign of her ritual. Even to her Grecian worshippers words were but faint symbols to express her truth. They saw, they felt her meaning, but they did not dishonor her by confining in empty phrases the secret of infinite Nature. Contrast the verbiage of Christian dogmatism! Hegel's vision of Eleusis ends in the ideal faith that the holy mystery is not irrecoverably lost.

> *Not on their lips didst thou, O Goddess, live;*
> *It was their lives that honored thee,*
> *And in their deeds thou livest still.*
> *Even this night I sensed thee, holy godhead.*
> *Thy children's life reveals thy truth to me,*
> *I see thee as the spirit of their acts.*
> *Thou art their high purport and loyal faith,*
> *The one divinity that wavers not, though all else fail.*[21]

THE RELIGION OF BEAUTY

In turning now to the thought of the mature Hegel on Greek civilization we enter a new world. The romantic mood of the "Eleusis" poem, the mood of longing after far-off ideals, has been supplanted by a sober, even hard realism. The influence of Hölderlin and young Schiller is gone. The *Phenomenology of Spirit* and all Hegel's later books and lectures are studded with merciless gibes at his Romantic idealist contemporaries, who found the garish world of everyday uncongenial and impossible. There are only harsh words for the subjectivity of Schiller's ideal of the *schöne Seele* and the formless and effeminate yearnings of Goethe's Werther. To a large extent Hegel's later system of thought represents a reaction against romantic *Fernweh*. The contemporary poet, Novalis, defined philosophy as "homesickness"; while Hegel considered it, as we saw in an earlier chapter, as being at home with oneself and one's world. This cool objective habit of taking things as they are had not been absent even in the youthful Hegel. Indeed Hölderlin at the height of their friendship at Tübingen had called him that "calm intellectualist" (ruhiger Verstandesmensch) and the epithet has seemed to many to be peculiarly appropriate. Though his writings are permeated with strong feeling, amounting at times to passion, there was within him an almost ruthless power of intellect which enabled him to rise above emotion and to survey the world, as did Spinoza, under the aspect of eternity.

The mood of the theological fragments had been characterized by the desire to have done with much of the recent German heritage. The more disillusioned temper of Hegel in his later years was not to reject, but to seek for the positive content in what was at hand. To be reconciled with his age, to desire nothing better than the present and what it offered, but to have this present in its best fulfilment—this became the avowed purpose of his life. It was the resolve and the conviction of the chastened Wilhelm Meister: here or nowhere is America. Hegel had come to believe that the dreams of a blissful primeval state of man, which so filled the minds of his German contemporaries, were a delusion and something of a snare as well. He now proceeded from a consciously modern standpoint, teaching that every man and every opinion is a product of the particular age, the people, and the society to which he or it belongs. To attempt to return to an older persuasion or religious faith, to warm up the old, is futile,—even impossible. The past, though not dead, has been superseded; and the problem is to live in the present, to make a vital peace with the real, and to concern oneself with living issues of the day. These emphases are constantly reiterated.

Young Hegel had been effective in discovering the contradictions and revealing the cultural problems at the root of contemporary society. The mature Hegel forged a metaphysical system, one of the most imposing and vast that man has ever conceived, in which all problems are caught up into a wider context and treated by a dialectic that veils all contradictions in synthesis. His intellectual longing for inclusiveness becomes henceforth his most characteristic trait. To account for all things and to make them all conform in an encyclopedic whole—this is the ambition of the Hegel with whom we now become acquainted. There is probably no one who has read his writings who has not been disturbed and rendered distrustful by this passion for unity where no unity seems possible. Because he yielded to this overmastering tendency to account for all phenomena and to weld together even the most conflicting aspects of history, serious thinkers have tended, ever since the first flush of enthusiasm of the early Hegelians died away, to regard his system as artificial and unreal.

Much has been written on the influence of the metaphysical system upon his historical interpretations. There can be no question that the application of his peculiar logic to historical development did affect that understanding. To attempt to comprehend the past in terms of thesis, antithesis, and synthesis, and to read all history as a necessary progress according to logical pattern could not fail to determine to some extent the values and the events he chose to find significant. Too often his historical judgments and keen empirical sense for the actual are sacrificed to the metaphysical scheme. The later Hegel gives constant evidence of the conflict within his own mind between his profound historical intuitions and the demands of his dialectic, a kind of doubleness that was to separate his followers into widely divergent camps.

On the other hand, it is no less true that the social, cultural motives of his philosophy were conceived long before they were reduced to the formulas in which they were systematically set forth. Hegel was a philosopher of history before he became a metaphysician. For this reason the relation of the dialectical structure to the historical content of his thought is not so close as has often been asserted. The problems that concerned young Hegel, problems suggested by his studies of European culture, are now elaborated within the confines of the metaphysical scheme. Though it would be futile to maintain that the system's needs remained without influence, it is nevertheless possible to consider the historical problems in relative independence of it. In a word, it is possible to follow the course of Hegel's early estimate of Hellenic culture as it develops through his later works, and it is to this that we shall turn in the following chapters.

In Hegel's system—his historical writings occupy the third division, which is called the *Philosophie des Geistes*—Hellenic civilization is seen in the context of other past epochs. The classical period is treated as a former stage in the phenomenology of the human spirit. With this subsumption of Hellenic culture, there goes a new doctrine of modern society, which accounts in large measure for the change in Hegel's attitude toward the Greeks between the period of the fragments and the later thought. Students of his development have been unanimous in remarking a gradual change that occurred in his writings in the early years of the nineteenth century, during the lectureship at Jena and the association with Schelling. It is particularly noteworthy in the shorter political treatises of this period which immediately precede the *Phenomenology of Spirit* and it is abundantly evident there.[1] In the earlier writings Hellenism had been to him, on the whole, the highest attainment yet realized in the ethical, indeed in all, cultural spheres. The whole period from the rise of the Roman empire to the present was considered a deterioration. The mysticism and world-weariness of Christian civilization seemed to him to indicate a defection from the vital humanistic ideals of Athenian life. At best the modern world appeared merely as a period of preparation for the readoption of Greek ethics and the Greek way of life. But from now on—that is, after the publication of the *Phenomenology of Spirit*—Hegel viewed Christian culture in a different light. He realized that it was not wholly decadent, but had contributed to humanity original and important values. Henceforth the present was looked upon, not as a falling away from past splendor, but as a higher synthesis of truths which the past had discovered. Whereas in his youth Hegel had appreciated only one great *Weltanschauung* in the history of human values, the mature philosopher added a second, which he broadly denominated as Christian. And he admitted that it was incumbent upon a realistic thinker to live in this second world. The Hellenic became a point of reference for the evaluation of Christian ideals and values.

Yet when this has been said and due emphasis placed on the changed viewpoint, it is true that Hegel always remained a rebel toward his immediate background and tradition. The loves and hates of his youth, the deep imprint of Greek studies, the dominant humanism that came to the fore in his first writings, colored his whole philosophy and determined its general outline. His mature philosophy, speaking generally, consisted of a modern content poured into Greek molds. In intellect, temperament and the dominant emphases of his teaching, he still seems closer to the Greek philosophers than to his fellow Germans. It is the irony of history that this man who now preached a doctrine of reconciliation between the present and the past should find himself so out of sympathy with many of the persuasions of his time. No more revealing indication of his preference for the Greeks could be found than a passage in the opening lecture on Greek philosophy, which Hegel delivered nearly every year till the day of his death. He tells there how the European mind has had to pass through a long discipline. The instruments of that discipline were Roman law and the Church. These two kept the impetuous, unrestrained European character in check, formed it, rendered its hardness pliable, and finally gave it "capacity for freedom". But, says Hegel,

> when man began to be at home with himself, he turned to the Greeks to find enjoyment in it. Let us leave the Latin and the Roman to the church and jurisprudence. Higher, freer philosophic science, and the beauty of untrammeled art, together with the taste and love of them, we know to have had their root in Greek life and to have derived from them their spirit. If we were permitted to have an aspiration, it would be for such a land and such conditions.[2]

In his young days Hegel had dealt little or not at all with Greek art. His judgments of religion appear to have been mainly derived from histories of Greece or from his reading of Plato. As a mature thinker, he became clearly aware of the role Greek sculpture and literature had played in Greek religion, as is shown in the *Philosophy of Fine Art* and the *Philosophy of Religion*. Though Hegel was conscious of the difference between art and religion—particularly in the modern world—his insistence that the two have common goals and express common universal truths is part of the emphasis of his metaphysical system. Hence in interpreting Greek art he constantly sought its religious basis, and subsumed both art and religion under the general categories of beauty and the ideal.

From the perspective of history, an explanation of the interconnection of Greek art and religion lay in the intellectual ferment of the Germany of one hundred and forty years ago. It is necessary for us to keep in mind Hegel's milieu in order to understand his vision of Greece. His age was dominated by intellectual leaders of artistic and poetic genius. They inherited the legacy of Winckelmann, the father of the neoclassical movement, the founder of a faith of which Lessing, Goethe, Wilhelm von Humboldt, Schiller, Hölderlin and many others were convinced adherents. These Hellenists did not look back to the Greece of Hesiod; they were almost unaware at first of the religion of the common people, that compound of superstition and magic in which modern scholars delve. For the most part they hardly saw the actual political or social history of Greece at all. Their attention was concentrated upon the great tragedies, Homer, the odes of Pindar, and above all, the then available remains of classic sculpture. The view which they obtained was in no sense complete. They saw an idealized Hellas, a picture of the few, the exceptional, the perfect.

But they were not wholly deluded. For the history of the neoclassical development in the Germany of this era from Winckelmann and Lessing to Schelling and Hegel presents a growing awareness of this idealization of Hellenism. The new religion that for a time pressed back Christianity and the German heritage was of intense but comparatively brief duration. Greece had appeared as a star in the night, but the dawn came all too soon, in the shape of nineteenth century political realities.[3]

Most of Winckelmann's disciples, however, preferred not to see the harder realities of Hellenic history. For them Greece remained an idealized vision. Had not Goethe written that among all the peoples of the world the Greeks dreamed the dream of life most beautifully? Toward the close of his life, even he surmised that this conviction was itself a dream, but he preferred to dream it to the end.

It was no common vision that had opened before these men of Germany. As they journeyed to Rome, to the sunny southland on the path of Winckelmann, to gaze upon magnificent classic fragments of gods and demi-gods, as they memorized their Homer and Sophocles, they were profoundly convinced that man had possessed in that ancient day a more central place in creation. He had latterly fallen from that higher and more glorious estate. The German past, their cultural heritage, had been permeated by the overwhelming sense of man's inadequacy before the majesty of the Divine. The world-denying aspect of Christianity had, indeed, loomed larger and had persisted in Germany longer than in other lands. This was why it meant something basic, something radical, for Germans to find a culture that placed man, not God in the center, and conceived his worth to lie not in dependence on transcendent deity, but in the degree of independence and self-sufficiency which he had himself attained. It seemed to this generation that man had in Greece reached the pinnacle of dignity and worth. The human form constituted the center of Greek art and the world of the Olympian divinities was itself only a plane higher than the human. Education was directed toward perfecting the human creature, to the transformation of his natural qualities and the cultivation of his powers.

It was preeminently the dream of a heightened and glorified humanity that these Hellenists envisaged in Greece. There were many for whom the Greek became a personal ideal of character as well. The qualities they most sought, the sense of totality, of wholeness and fulness of experience, were found in the great Greek individuals. *Sophrosyne,* which connoted for them both fulness and harmony, seemed the basic characteristic of Greek life. Winckelmann compressed his lifelong study of Greek art into a brief utterance that became the *Leitwort* of the movement: *edle Einfalt, stille Grösse,* noble simplicity, serene greatness. "As the depths of the sea remain constantly calm, however much the surface may rage, so do the lineaments of the Greek statues express, despite all passions, a great and tranquil soul." The image that soared before their minds, Hegel's along with the rest, was that of the great individual, the Apollo among men, who could stand superior to the vicissitudes of time and circumstance. It was what Goethe tried to express and exemplify in the ideal of *Ruhe in der Bewegung,* "Rest in movement", and *Dauer im Wechsel,* "The permanent amid change". The Greece that Winckelmann discovered and knew stood under the sign of Apollo, which connoted serenity, *theoria,* godlike wisdom.

But all this time there was growing up, within the very ranks of this same generation, and not always clearly separated from it, a new force and a new emphasis that sought and found quite different values in the ancient world. This was the newer Romantic school which arose as a kind of offset to the neoclassical ideal. Its beginning was in the *Sturm und Drang* reaction against the narrow rationalism of the Enlightenment. For it nature was inexhaustible and the genius, *der Genie,* must explore it all. The ideal was not the plastic, self-contained individual, but a boundless catholicity. The man to be admired was not the character who exemplified harmony within clear, fixed outlines, but the man who could live in any world and find not peace but more experience. And because the Romanticists kept discovering new ideals to worship, their interest in past history likewise changed. They perceived the "night side" of Greek life. Prometheus was their symbol, not Apollo; Penthesilea and Medea replaced Iphigenia and Helen. Their religiosity explored the cults of Orphic and Pythagorean mysteries. More than that, in their troubled needs, these Romanticists went further back than Greece to the Orient, especially to India and Egypt, and found in these obscure but varicolored civilizations elements still closer to their spirit than even Dionysian Greece. Klopstock and, to some degree, Novalis began to direct attention to the world of symbol and allegory of the Christian Middle Ages. Apollonian Greece grew pale as the light was shifted to Indian and Christian images. Friedrich Schlegel exemplifies well this Romantic trend though many others could be named. He had taken up promiscuously Oriental, classical and medieval elements, and to a remarkable degree his life and opinions mirror these heterogeneous influences.

Such, in general, were the two points of view, not always distinct, in regard to classical Greece, to which the philosopher Hegel sought to bring clarity and understanding. His sympathies were on the side of Winckelmann and Goethe, and his delineation of Hellenic art and religion developed in conscious opposition to the clouded ideals of the Romanticists. Though he brought a wider and fuller knowledge of historical facts to balance his interpretation than did any of the others, it is not difficult to see the prevailing influence of the neoclassic school. While his vision of Greece did not fade, the inherent values of Christian philosophy more and more asserted themselves and demanded consideration. In this development Hegel had much in common with his contemporaries.

But he differed in one central emphasis. Herder, von Humboldt, Hölderlin and others were inclined to see Greek art and ethical values in the light of a new Germany, to stress the likeness of the two peoples, and uphold the possibility of a new Periclean age. They hoped for a palingenesis of spirit, a rebirth of Greece in Germany. Goethe both as a personality and as an artist towered before many German eyes as a great Greek pagan, a figure out of the Hellenic pantheon. Many looked to him as harbinger of a new day. Not so Hegel. His interpretation of Greece arose, as we have seen, not out of a sense of its likeness to his own age, but out of a sharp antithesis. The classic world was dead, palingenesis impossible. He believed that antiquity had gone to ruin on the very principles for which the modern age stood, and though he was far from approving many of those principles, he was certain that they were different from those of Greece. The problem was one of understanding and appropriating rather than of imitating or reviving Greek naturalistic ideals. He quoted with approval the famous conclusion of Schiller's poem on "die Götter Griechenlands":

> *Wrested from the flood of Time's abysses,*
> *Saved, they float above high Pindus now;*
> *All that was immortal life within them*
> *Lives in song, all other life must go.*[4]

As a starting point and basis for understanding Greece Hegel found primary significance in the sentence of Herodotus that Homer and Hesiod gave the Greeks their gods, their religion. What could that mean except that poets and artists had been their very teachers and seers? Prophecy in Greece was poetry. When the Greeks had early sought explanation of natural phenomena by reference to spiritual powers, artistic imagination had answered their questions with the myth that all things were full of gods. Homer and Hesiod had given them an explanation of the world. Their medium was not reflection but imagination. The gods arose out of their fancy, out of the stuff of their experience and their creative life.

Hegel felt that modern men were too likely to assume from this that the gods were merely invented or thought up as a likely explanation. The religion of Greecé did not grow out of the isolated individual experience of the poets, but out of a general experience rooted in the spirit and faith of the people and the age. Hegel insisted that artistic fancy can in no sense be thought equivalent to what is commonly considered fictional. The Greek gods were not fictitious but poetic creations, *nicht erdichtet, sondern gedichtet*—and that makes a great difference.

It was in this conception of fancy as the medium of explanation of the natural that Hegel found the essential Greek spirit. The true Greek attitude was the artistic attitude: the habit of transforming the outer and external into a work of art, a product of beauty and usefulness. The dispute among scholars in the Germany of Hegel's later years as to the foreign origin of the Greek gods was to him insignificant and meaningless. Early German scholars had shown that Herodotus' history contained a basic contradiction on this very important question. In one place "the father of history" wrote that Homer and Hesiod had created his people's theogony, but later he pointed out that most of the gods were of foreign origin, and had Egyptian prototypes. In the early years of the nineteenth century German scholars laboriously established this second assertion of Herodotus. Creuzer, especially, laid the basis for this leading theme of future research.

Hegel accepted and acknowledged Creuzer's work, but found far more significant the un-Egyptian function and character that these divinities assumed in Greece. Herodotus, he held, would have been astonished had he been told that his two statements contained a contradiction. For the artistic spirit of the Greeks had needed and used the foreign only as a stimulus and raw material upon which to work. The finished product was peculiarly and entirely their own. That was basic in their religion of beauty: it was a work of art, a creation of the human spirit. Greek art and religion were the work of man and as such were individual and particular, but not at all subjective and arbitrary in what was to Hegel the erroneous modern sense. Gods were the work of men, yet no less divine and no less venerated for that reason. The Greeks, as artists, recognized the gods whom they formed as their own product, yet did them honor as something more than themselves, as substantially and objectively valid. The gods were at the same time man's innate will and objective powers. The Greek artist could fashion gods in plastic form and yet know that his work was more than he.

He has a respect and veneration for these conceptions and images— this Olympian Zeus—this Pallas of the Acropolis—and in the same way for the laws, political and ethical, that guide his actions. But he, the human being, is the womb that conceived them, he the breast that suckled them, he the spiritual to which their grandeur and purity are owing. Thus he feels himself calm in contemplating them, and not only free in himself, but possessing the consciousness of his freedom; thus the honor of the human is swallowed up in the worship of the divine. Men honor the divine in and for itself, but at the same time as their deed, their production, their phenomenal existence; thus the divine receives its honor through the respect paid to the human and the human in virtue of the honor paid to the divine.[5]

In Hegel's opinion it was the stage of individuality which the Greeks had attained that made the perfect level for beautiful production. The moderns were inferior to them in the sphere of artistic creation. Schiller had written an essay, entitled *Über naive und sentimentalische Dichtung*, in which he developed the idea that there were two fundamental classes of poetry or art, corresponding to two types of artists. There was the naive artist who lived in immediate and harmonious union with nature, to whom the conflict of medium and significance of art had not come, and who was capable of so complete a surrender to the object that life and art became an organic whole. On the other hand, there was the reflective artist, for whom art and life were in disjunction. Thought had brought him into conflict with immediacy; his material was intractable and unequal to the spiritual import of his idea. To use Schiller's own metaphor, the reflective, sentimental artist and man had lost nature and needed to set out on the painful search for it. He had fallen from the paradise of the natural and longed for reconciliation and return. Art represented a struggle for harmony, and was less a natural than a self-conscious and artificial product. Schiller considered the Greek artist the basic exemplar of naive poetry, the modern as representing the reflective and sentimental.

In this Hegel agreed with Schiller, though he preferred to put the distinction in slightly different terms. The Greek's view of nature separated him from both the Oriental and the modern. To understand the relationship between nature and the human spirit is to understand what Hegel meant by characterizing this civilization as "the mean of beauty". The Greek as artist could not view the world about him as foreign or indifferent. He felt an intimation of confidence in it, a feeling that this natural world afforded material for his spiritual home. Wonder and presentiment were the comprehensive categories which Hegel used to describe this attitude. The Greeks watched nature and surmised regarding her. Everything must have a human and comprehensible meaning. Out of wonder and surmise rose the beautiful world of Greek mythology. From "that thrill which pervades us in the silence of the forests" came the concept of Pan. The fountains were the origin of the Muses. Nature communicated with man, answering the questions which he put to her. Yet the answers were the product of his own spirit, which found in the external, material for its own creative fancy. "The immortal songs of the Muses are not that which is heard in the murmuring of the fountains; they are the productions of the thoughtfully listening spirit—creative while observant."[6]

Hegel thought it difficult for a modern German to understand the central role of beauty in Greek life. Nature and spirit were not in opposition in the great figures of sculpture, nor in the historic personages of Herodotus or Thucydides. The Greeks had found a harmony, not as some of the Oriental peoples had done by disregarding spiritual forces and allowing the natural to rule. Nor had they sought it as the modern Christian world had tried to do, by disregarding and suppressing the natural. Kant asserted that the individual attained full stature only by putting down the natural and the sensuous, and by behaving in accordance with rational law. The religious tradition likewise encouraged a rigid and discordant dualism. Man became wholly man only through rejection of component elements of his natural self. The external world as well as his own desires made demands upon him which he could not fulfil. Driven within the confines of his subjective self, he attempted to determine the external out of himself and his private convictions.

Hegel believed that the Greeks of the Periclean age had not experienced the dissonance of inner and outer which he felt to be the central cleavage in modern life. They came before his vision as having achieved a mean of beauty. They had found harmony between nature and spirit by making nature the instrument of their purposes, by bringing it into the service of their spirit, not by despising but by revering it as the basis and foundation of all. And this harmony of form and content, of spirit and nature, was always an objective and explicit harmony, a union for all to see—spirit given concrete form in the natural, the natural given transformed expression in the spiritual. Hegel compresses what he means by this harmony of the Hellenic soul into a fine metaphor.

The Greek spirit is the plastic artist, forming the stone into a work of art. In this formative process the stone does not remain mere stone—the form being only superinduced from without; but it is made an expression of the spiritual, even contrary to its nature, and thus transformed. Conversely, the artist needs for his spiritual conceptions, stone, colors, sensuous forms to express his idea. Without such an element he can no more be conscious of the idea himself than give it an objective form for the contemplation of others; since it cannot in thought alone become an object to him.[7]

"From out of thy passions, O man, hast thou derived the materials for thy gods," spoke an ancient sage. The words seemed to Hegel to reveal something basic about the Hellenic religion of beauty. The world of Greek deities had grown out of the passions of the Greek artist. Many passions had made their home in the breast of man, and many gods had been formed therefrom. Hegel's analysis of the nature of art led him to assert that it was primarily concerned with bringing forth spiritual ideals and rendering them visible to sense. And since the artistic spirit ruled in Greek life, these passions of men had given rise to gods formed into the character of ideals. This is an essential theme in his interpretation of Greek religion and art. He conceived Greek life in its flower to have been ruled to a unique extent by the conception of the ideal. The ideal! That was the magic word that concerned Schiller so closely, and to which he looked for release from the unhappy dualisms of *Sinnenglück und Seelenfriede*. In his philosophical poems he had given expression to the surmise that the dominance of ideals made the harmony and totality of Greek life possible. Hegel expanded and developed Schiller's concept in relation to the contemporary scene and Schiller's own longing. To the modern man, according to Hegel, an ideal involved something unattainable, a vision in the clouds—not something latent in the nature of things as they are. It connoted even an opposition to the real and the existent, thus assuming the character of a *mere* ideal. To his Romantic contemporaries, he felt, it was forever an object of vain striving, of indistinct yearning for a world beyond the temporal and prosaic —the delightful but pathetic dream-world of Hölderlin's wistful odes. Hegel, foe of all frustrations and dualisms, believed that he found in the Greeks a freer and truer conception of the ideal as a spiritualization of the natural and the real. To have an ideal in that world was to realize it, to embody it, to give it form. The ideal was a sane vision of the possibilities of life when freed of accidental irrelevancies. The essential nature of the Greek gods thus came to full and adequate expression in their sculpture. For they were no more than spiritualized ideals, expressing in essential form traits which the Greeks considered most characteristic and desirable in human life.

These ideal figures of Greek religion were concrete individualities. The Greeks had no place for abstractions. The formless, the unclear, the indefinite they could not endure. They shuddered at the vast and limitless imagination of the Oriental. Hegel cites the myth of the punishment meted out to the Titans as a revelation of what they most detested.

> These punishments are, in truth, the false type of infinity, the yearning of the indefinite aspiration or the unsatisfied craving of natural desires, which in their eternal repetition fail to discover rest or final satisfaction. For the truly godlike intuition of the Greeks regarded the mere extension into space and the region of the indefinite, not, as some modern votaries of such longings do, as the highest attainment of mankind, but as a damnation which it relegates to Tartarus.[8]

Because he believed in the artistic unity of real and ideal in the Greek spirit, Hegel vigorously opposed the early nineteenth century interpretation of the symbolical nature of the Greek gods. Creuzer's work on *Symbolik und Mythologie*, which appeared in four volumes between 1812-1816, had become a sort of bible to the Romanticists, as Winckelmann's work had been to the neoclassicists. There the attempt was made, not only to trace the Asiatic origin of Greek divinities, but to interpret them symbolically, as representations of either natural or abstract human powers. The idea of symbolism had a great appeal to Hegel's Romantic contemporaries. Friedrich Schlegel asserted that all art was symbolic by its very nature, that it was merely an inadequate sign of an inexpressible reality. Hegel, the intellectual and philosopher, opposed this theory, especially in its application to the representation of the Hellenic deities. In his judgment, the Orient had been dominated by symbol. There the human spirit had been incapable of expressing itself adequately either in sensuous forms or in clear concepts. In his *Vorlesungen über die Ästhetik* he used the general term 'symbolical' to characterize all Oriental art. For Asia had been dominated by a sense of the inadequacy of the outer to represent the inner, of form to delineate content. Nothing in this art ever carried its meaning stamped on its face; one always needed a key to understand the meaning.

This, for Hegel, in contrast to most of his contemporaries, was the source of weakness of the Oriental, not its strength. The symbol by its very nature, he taught, is ambiguous and abstract; it can always mean more than one thing, since many abstract qualities can be represented by a single symbol. Hegel thought that the Oriental world had never arrived at a clear determination of its own nature, and of what it wanted to say. To his Romantic contemporaries Hegel opposed his own ideal in challenging terms.

> **Only that which is spiritual imperatively demands the light; and that which does not reveal itself and in itself expound its own interpretation**

is the unspiritual which fades again once more into night and obscurity. That which is of spirit on the contrary reveals itself, and purifies itself, by itself defining its external form, from the caprice of the imagination, the flood of obstructing shapes, and the otherwise perturbed accessories of symbolical sense.[9]

Hegel realized that his own philosophic convictions were out of harmony with the then existing state of art. Modern artists inevitably found form inadequate to express content. So they turned to symbols, to ambiguity and to abstraction. Though Hegel granted that this was actually the case with contemporary artists and though he wanted to find a justification for it within art's realm, he was no less certain that such had not been the case with the Greeks. For them significance and form had been perfectly wedded, and the sculptured gods expressed exactly what they were. It is difficult to overemphasize this conviction in Hegel's interpretation of the Greeks or its importance in determining his own philosophy. This Greek world represented to him the precise opposite of romantic indeterminacy and mystic absorption. The Greeks loved the specific; their gods were concrete idealizations of actual human characters. These beings who were recognized and honored as substantial powers expressed what they meant and meant only what was expressed.

The Muse is herself the composition of poetry; Athene herself is Athenian life. . . . These powers rule in as immanent a way in the reality with which they are connected as the laws act within the planets.[10]

To this insistence on the concrete and the immanent Hegel related the sense of joy and celebration with which religious festivals were observed in Attica. The deep dissatisfaction of his boyhood with the too foreign and austere character of traditional Christianity never really left him. Though his attitude toward the Christian faith in his later lectures on the *Philosophy of Religion* had radically changed, there still remained a core of revolt against Christianity's negative and otherworldly aspects. Hegel's bent was always away from world-denial and toward participation and enjoyment. Few philosophers have possessed such enduring optimism, few have been so completely positive in their total philosophy.

This is especially evident in Hegel's conception of the function of religion. In the theological meditations of his youth worship had been central, and it was still central in his mature system. Worship was the union of universal and particular, the coming together of God and man. Deity descended from on high and man ascended from his limited estate. Worship is "a continuous poetry of life", not service in any menial sense, as the

German word *Gottesdienst* might imply. For the Greeks, religion did not lift only one aspect of human life to divine status; it lifted the whole of existence. The divine, as the hypostatization of ideals, had been for them inherently connected with the real and existent.

That is the source of the deep attraction which this people and their religion of beauty possessed for the German philosopher. Christian faith was born in an epoch of history characterized by the deep cleft between the real world and men's ideals. Religion was for Roman Christians a necessary bond, a sustaining and comforting refuge. Hegel felt that this was foreign to the Periclean Greeks. Need had not created their theogony. There was no salvation for man because none was necessary. Within his own sphere man was supreme and though the inexorable powers of necessity had the final word, they were not moved by man's wishes. He paid them reverent homage, not because of his need, but out of his abundance, a worship not caused by fear and not mixed with tears.

> This religion is essentially a religion of humanity, that is, the concrete man, as regards what he actually is, as regards his needs, inclinations, passions, and habits, as regards his moral and political relations, and in reference to all that has value in these and is essential, is in his gods in presence of his own nature. Or, to put it otherwise, his god has within him the very content composed of the noble and the true, which is at the same time that of concrete man. . . . In this religion there is nothing incomprehensible, nothing which cannot be understood; there is no kind of content in the god which is not known to man, or which he does not find and know in himself. The confidence of a man in the gods is at the same time his confidence in himself.[11]

Such was Hegel's mature estimate of Greek religion. In broad outlines it agrees with the interpretation of the whole neoclassic movement. For Hegel it involved denial of the importance of the mystery religions. Orphic, Pythagorean, Eleusinian cults in which modern scholars find significant indications of other tendencies of Hellenic life, he considered as mere Asiatic survivals. They represented for him a return of the Greek spirit to its beginnings, before the natural gods, the Titans, had been overcome by Zeus and his hierarchy. In spite of his early poem on Eleusis, Hegel later insisted that the Athenians set no real store by their official mystery, since they were well aware that the true reconciliation of divine and human could not rest in symbol or secrecy.

It would, however, be unfair to Hegel's final meaning to stop here. In developing the Greek view of life against a background of modern ideals which he opposed, it often appears as if he were giving wholehearted approval to the Greeks. But he knew that there was in all Greek life a pathetic, defeated element. The world had advanced since then; Christianity had brought a new doctrine of man, a great hope for the individual which if rightly understood gave the modern man immense superiority over the ancient. In discussing the Greek view of tragedy and its relation to necessity Hegel brings out most clearly the difference between the pagan and Christian *Weltanschauungen*.

As we have seen, the German neoclassicists were fascinated by the serenity of the great personages, divine and human, of the ancient world. For Hegel, too, these ideal figures represented a measure of self-sufficiency and lofty calm unattainable in modern times. He explained this by the different claims that the two ages made upon mankind. Unlike modern men, the Greeks made no absolute demand that the world be conformable to their will. They recognized the sphere of their own dominion, and a sphere that was not theirs. In such limitation they had found the way to dominion over things and over themselves. Hegel believed that the serenity of the Greeks which appealed so strongly to the struggling Germans, arose out of a deep-seated conviction that things are so and that the individual must be content. Man could be free only within limits, limits which he must accept with finality and if possible with joy. Inexorable necessity ruled over men and gods alike.

Hegel interpreted necessity, like everything else in Greek life, as having gone through a process of development. In the Homeric epics fate is blind, but in the great tragedies of the Periclean age this concept is replaced by the idea of the rationality of fate. The whole basis upon which the tragic conflict turned was, in Hegel's view, the rationality and intelligibility of the outcome. The collision which gave rise to ancient tragedy—and in this interpretation Hegel was thinking of Aeschylus and Sophocles, not, generally, of Euripides—was a conflict between objective ethical powers. This conflict resolved itself into the opposition of a limited or family code to the more universal requirements of the state. The struggle was not, as in modern tragedy, within the individual character or characters; it was a conflict between objective spiritual powers.

The pathos of this conflict arose from the fact that both opposing parties were right in their own sphere, but both were inevitably one-sided. Absolute justice decreed that both alike should fail in the interests of the ethical order as a whole. The individual, representing special interests, colliding with a totality of forces, of things that are, must necessarily perish. But in the individual's destruction the total rational order triumphs. Devotion to a single ideal, good in itself, but imperfect in the light of the rest of life, brings catastrophe for the agent. The outcome cannot be individual triumph. The objective whole asserts its right over the partial. "To such clearness of insight and of artistic presentation", writes Hegel, "did Greece attain at her highest stage of culture."

In this interpretation of ancient tragedy Hegel approached an essential motif of his own philosophy. The individual cannot measure himself against the objective whole; he cannot assert freedom by opposing, but by bringing his will into harmony with the real. Injustice arises only when the person places his own will and his subjective conviction in opposition to the ethical totality which determines him. Individual will is alone the irrational, for it stands in isolation and detachment.

What Hegel considered to be the insufficiency and inadequacy in the Greek religion of beauty is preeminently revealed in this conception of tragedy. He saw it as the explanation of the negative, the consolatory basis of a major part of Greek life. This was the reason why Plato could make Socrates say: "We are, after all, like children crying in the dark." This force of absolute necessity or absolute justice that conditioned pagan life, though it made for serenity, also carried within it an infinite sadness. For, in the last analysis, there was no hope. Man was as nothing; the world was all. Justice carried nothing of the human within its deadly abstractness. For Hegel the Christian story replaced that conception of justice with the myth of God the Father, of whom man was the son and bore his Father's image. Christian philosophy and the modern civilization into which it was woven had surpassed the negative character of the older cult, and had conceived of redemption and life in the spirit as a second nature. The serenity which was ideally possible here was built on pain, but the consequent reconciliation carried with it a wholly positive content. Christian serenity was born not of renunciation, but of union with God.

Hegel—if I understand his meaning—wanted to retain in its main outline the Greek conception with its emphasis on the social, the concrete, the objective and the vital. These made a powerful appeal, and were needed in a modern Christianity where sacred and secular were too often distinct. Yet he desired a fuller and more adequate picture than the Greeks had seen. Man should behold not a world of irreconcilable necessity, but one ruled by love and forgiveness, where the human being is not a creature of nature, but a member of the kingdom of God. Greek tragedy could resolve conflict only by the individual's destruction, only by an equalization in which deeds were effaced. Modern tragedy could end by reconciliation and atonement in which the individual, though he might lose his life, would not lose all, but could know the justice of his fate, and see in it the triumph of a larger value.

This new and important truth of Christianity meant, in terms of Hegel's formal philosophy, an advance from the level of beauty to that of thought, from art to philosophy. Greek religion, as a product of creative fancy, could not bear the scrutiny of thought and reflection. Christianity, on the other hand, was a faith to be grasped and known by reason, while at the same time it proved adequate to human passions and human desires. Such had been the advance in self-consciousness. Religion no longer required sensuous embodiment, or gods of marble. Mankind had become capable of worshipping God as spirit.

> In the earliest beginnings of art we shall find mystery still present, a secret strain and longing which persists because Art's imaginative powers are unable to envisage to sense the complete truth of its content. When once, however, the mind of man has succeeded in endowing such content with perfect outward shape in art, it is driven inevitably away from this objective realization to its own free spiritual activity as from something repellent to it. A period such as this is our own. We may, indeed, express the hope that art will rise to yet higher grades of technical perfection; but in any case Art in its specific form has ceased to meet the highest requirements of spiritual life. We may still wonder at the unrivalled excellence of the statues of the gods of Hellas, and imagine that God the Father, Christ, and the Virgin Mary have received ideal representation at the hands of more recent painters. But it is of no use. Our knees no longer bow to them.[12]

Thus, concluded Hegel, the inadequacy of Greek religion lay in the sphere of art itself. It could not express the last and final truth of man's own worth. The Greeks had been supreme in the realm of art: "there can be nothing more beautiful." The Christian God, however, could not be given form in marble, nor could the truths concerning man's destiny which are revealed in Him be adequately presented in sensuous form. For this, the medium of modern art was inadequate, and inevitably so. The dissonance of form and content, or of nature and spirit, which characterized the modern in contrast to the classical artist, resulted from the advance in self-consciousness, to the level at which the idea or ideal surpassed graphic representation. Modern artists needed symbolism as a means of expressing greater truth by signification and suggestion. This symbolism was not, to be sure, the symbolism of ancient Eastern art, where the ideal itself was as yet unprobed and ambiguous, and where the spirit was shrouded in nature.

Romantic symbolism was an implicit confession that the spiritual ideal, in its furthest reach, had advanced beyond art's confines.

Goethe had said, "The highest cannot be spoken." Hegel would have taken that to be the essential spirit of the modern artist. For the Greeks the highest could be spoken and was spoken in their art. For Hegel, too, unlike the artist, the highest could be spoken, but the language of this utterance was not art but philosophy.

THE HELLENIC SOCIAL ETHOS

Hegel's evaluation of the Hellenic social ethos can perhaps be most clearly understood if it is again sharply contrasted with the individualistic ideal of the Enlightenment and the views of Kant and Fichte. Broadly speaking, they interpreted social life from the standpoint of the ego and individual morality. To Hegel the doctrine of an individual imperative for conduct represented the cause of his people's political tragedy. The failure of the Germans to build a national state and develop a vital culture was, he thought, largely attributable to their excessive individualism, which had been accentuated in his own day by the reaction of Romantic subjectivity in the direction of mystical religion and by Kant's insistence on personal moral autonomy. Far apart as these two currents sometimes appeared to flow, they converged to carry the individual to a place where he could assume the role of supreme arbiter of history. Against this tendency Hegel set his ideal of a social ethos developed from the Greek *polis*. Though he had no wish to replace the positive advances of modern times by a retreat to antiquity, he believed that the painful contradictions of his own day and of his own people could be overcome by a synthesis of social ethics with individualism.

For Hegel the individual was determined by social institutions, the family, church, school, habits of community, and state. He did not "form the world out of himself" but was formed by the social world, transformed from a creature of impulse and nature into a spiritual, a rational being. Even his conscience, which Kant and Fichte held to be the sole spring of moral action, Hegel understood as chiefly the product of social training and habit. Objective, concrete institutions, bodies of custom and systems of law were a "second nature", resulting from man's struggle to give form and permanence to the requirements of his being. As such they represented the higher reaches of self-consciousness and reflection. Each rising generation, the children who were to perpetuate and develop these social patterns, first found their intellectual and moral habits determined by them. Through the process of education and discipline, this living heritage was built into their life. Ethical duties were mainly determined not from within but from without; they were not unique but habitual, not created but discovered.

Such, in brief, was Hegel's ethical insistence and though there were some who agreed with him, he was keenly aware that this doctrine was essentially foreign to his people. It was a wisdom that the Greeks had known. His was a day of individualism, subjectivity, Romantic passion for the creative, the personal, and the unique. The doctrine of the individual had given rise to a modern ethics which included higher truth than the ancients had known, but also contained the possibility of abstractness and abuse. Hegel summarized the different conceptions under the terms *Moralität* (individual morality), the principle of the modern; and *Sittlichkeit* (social, customary ethics), the characteristic of the Hellenic world.

In common with the other early Hellenists, Hegel saw Greek culture as a unity to an extent which modern research has made impossible for us. But in drawing his picture of the Hellenic ethical consciousness, he looked exclusively at Athens, Athens of the fifth century, the Periclean Age. Here the brief blossom of Greek ethical life was at its fairest. Here Hegel found the individual and the social will at one. The synthesis had been aided by pressure from without. The harmony of Athens under Pericles had been won in conflict with the opposing principles that formed the substance of the Asiatic world.

As the Christian world was distinguished from the Greek by a different conception of the individual, so the Greeks were distinguished from the Oriental by a different doctrine of man. Classical antiquity, standing between Orient and Occident, was, in Hegel's mythology, the bridge of the World-Spirit, on which civilization passed from East to West. Here he found the happy mean between the Oriental underemphasis of the individual and the excessive subjectivity of the modern Christian world. But the Greeks represented, from the perspective of their day, not a mediation between extremes, but a contrast and opposition, intellectual and physical, to the civilizations of the East. It is not mere chance, writes Hegel, that the two great heroic figures in Greek life, Achilles and Alexander, one the "ideal youth of poetry", the other "the ideal youth of reality", they with whom Greek civilization began and closed, were both arrayed against Asia.

As was said before, Hegel draws a sharp contrast between Greek and Oriental art, religion, and ideals of government. To the vast and formless striving of Asia, the Greeks opposed their bounded, finite and harmonious ideal. To the abstract and symbolic monism of Oriental religious concepts, the Greeks opposed a concrete and humanistic polytheism. To Oriental despotism and absolutism in government, the Greeks opposed a democratic and popular ideal. Hegel thought of the Egyptian spirit as representing a final development of the Oriental consciousness, before the birth pangs of the Western world. Everything in Egypt presented itself as a problem. The inscription over the temple of the goddess Neith is typical: "I am that which is, that which was, and that which will be; no one has lifted my veil." To this problematic, night-loving divinity the Greek Apollo, god of light and clarity, made answer: "Man, know thyself." This conflict of cultural principles, represented in the great wars with Persia, fused the Greek world into unity, and made the Athenians thrillingly conscious of their national destiny.

As Hegel's appraisal of Greek culture was derived from the Periclean synthesis, so his picture of the Hellenic social ethos was chiefly drawn from an equally limited field: the tragic dramas of Aeschylus and Sophocles. As early as his schoolboy days at Stuttgart, he had learned Greek well enough to attempt to translate Sophocles and there are few of his later books and lectures that do not contain Sophoclean references. When he characterized Greek ethics for his students the tragic drama was always his first source.

Commentators have not failed to call attention to the romantic idealization contained in material drawn from such sources. To describe Athens in this way is roughly comparable to a portrayal of the German ethos in the eighteenth century drawn from the writings of Klopstock or Lessing or Schiller. That does not mean that Hegel's portrayal of the *schöne Sittlichkeit* of the Greeks was entirely unrealistic. The Athenian dramatists did represent the ethical ideals of their time and people, however far short of those ideals the common practice may have been. And it must be remembered that Hegel's understanding of the past always took shape in terms of ideal values.

One Greek drama in particular was a favorite with Hegel all his life. As a work of art alone, it became for him the supreme masterpiece. When he wanted to show concretely some inclusive aspect of the Hellenic ethical ideal, Hegel always turned to Antigone—"that noblest of figures that ever appeared on earth". There is, to be sure, a certain sentimentalism in this, but Hegel saw in Antigone's defiance of her king's commands a quality that was basic to her people's ethical consciousness. The laws, she says, which I obey are the immutable unwritten laws of Heaven.

> *They were not born today nor yesterday;*
> *They die not; and none knoweth whence they sprang.*
> (F. Storr's translation)

Laws that are not of today or of yesterday! Laws that must be obeyed at whatever cost to one's own life and despite the wrong of disobedience to a state decree! This was Greek piety, piety toward the unwritten religious compulsions of family and tribe. Reliance on custom and tradition avoided the one-sidedness and fanaticism of modern individualistic motivation. In his polemic against Kant and Fichte it is this ideal of respect and veneration and obedience to the inherited code that is held up as the indispensable basis of every moral action.

But Antigone represented only one side of Greek ethical consciousness. The other side is personified in Kreon. The tragic collision grows out of the conflict of family piety and state authority. Kreon, lawful successor to the throne of Thebes, forbade the burial of the rebellious Polynices, killed in a fratricidal conflict for his father's throne. As traitor Polynices had forfeited all claims, and Kreon exercised the state's authority. But Polynices' sister, Antigone, impelled by all the religious and natural family bonds of the ages, violated the law, performed the sacred duty and was required to expiate her crime by death.

Here we have both the tragic conflict and a revelation of Greek ethical values as Hegel understood them. On the one hand, there are the individual and family relationships, founded on the basis of natural association and propinquity. Communal ties rule here. Out of such bonds springs the elemental but vital religious consciousness. On the other hand, there is the larger community, the nation, whose interests and will have become unified in the state. Though the state is not essentially antithetical to the family unit, their interests occasionally clash. But this clash cannot be regarded as a struggle between a religious and a secular ethic. The state embodies religious values in their more universal and rational form; its gods are more than the family gods. The Hellenic city-state incorporated a more self-conscious and spiritual level of substantial morality than that which existed in the smaller family group. Greek civil law was an advance over tribal regulations and represented a widening of allegiance, a progress beyond the natural. Just as the love between sister and brother, according to Hegel, is a higher ethical bond than that between father and son or husband and wife because there is no natural necessity which requires it, so the duty to society or the state is a higher duty than allegiance to kin or tribe.

In this interpretation, Kreon and Antigone both epitomize essential ethical values. But they stand for different levels of Greek *Sittlichkeit*. Antigone represents the natural basis of the social ethos, Kreon its more developed range. In the drama both must perish. The two sides have both become involved in conflict and it is necessary for the ethical whole to triumph rather than that either part should win. But it is important to realize that Kreon stands for the more rational level of ethical consciousness. Antigone

relied on the law of the gods. The gods, however, whom she thus revered, are the Dei inferi of Hades, . . . the instinctive powers of feeling, love and kinship, not the daylight gods of free and self-conscious, social and political life.[1]

Hegel saw the same conflict in most of the other dramas of Sophocles and Aeschylus. Each element was justified in its own sphere. It was not that the more immediate and natural was evil in itself, or that it was so regarded by the dramatist, but in relation to the demands of the larger society the claims of the family were less rational, because less universal, and in the case of conflict the lower claim must yield.

Though aware of this inherent dualism, Hegel nevertheless held up the Greek social ethos as a unified and harmonious whole. Its good was not some concept of moral duty that necessarily opposed desire, instinct and impulse, but it was a living ideal that arose out of a natural transmutation of the material of human relationships. That was for him the great value in the Greek view of life: it was built on a sane perception of the intrinsic connection between the ideal and the real, and it concerned itself little with impossible hopes of what man ought to be.

What was the origin of this ideal of right, this fusion of natural and spiritual values in Periclean Athens? Hegel would answer: It came from an imaginative consciousness of the past. In his lectures on the *History of Philosophy*, he described at considerable length Greek fondness for explaining what their past had been, for objectifying and revering it.

They represent their existence as an object apart from themselves, which manifests itself independently and which in its independence is of value to them; hence they have made for themselves a history of everything which they have possessed and have been. Not only have they represented the beginning of the world—that is, of gods and men, the earth, the heavens, the wind, mountains and rivers—but also of all aspects of their existence, such as the introduction of fire and the offerings connected with it, the crops, agriculture, the olive, horse, marriage, property, laws, arts, worship, the sciences, towns, princely races, etc. Of all these it is pleasingly represented through tales how they have arisen in history as their own work.[2]

This vital consciousness of their past, this living tradition had, as we saw, tremendously impressed young Hegel in his first acquaintance with the Greeks. And it is this characteristic that ultimately determined the older Hegel's estimate of their ethical consciousness. To be a Greek, above all, a Greek citizen, meant accepting a whole pattern of life, the positive product of a long development, guided and sustained by a sense of law. And what seemed so important to this nineteenth-century German was the Hellenic ideal of public life, which followed upon the consciousness of objective law. This was in complete contrast with the German romantic desire for seclusion, for privacy, for loneliness. Pericles, who had renounced private life altogether and devoted his genius wholly to the public good, remained in Hegel's vision the finest exemplification of the Athenian ideal. It was this Pericles who said that a man who takes no interest in public affairs is to be regarded not as a harmless but as a useless character.

To esteem his state and society before a private good was not for the citizen of Periclean Athens an abstract or artificial patriotism. This society had formed him and made him what he was. The Greeks had no word for "conscience"; nor did they know the modern principle of "the good will". Their conception of the good was formed by participation in society and their idea of virtue grew out of society's ideals. Hegel remarks that

> the consideration of the state in the abstract—which to our understanding is the essential point—was alien to them. Their grand object was their country in its living and real aspect; *this actual Athens*, this Sparta, these temples, these altars, this form of social life, this union of fellow citizens, these manners and customs. To the Greek his country was a necessity of life, without which existence was impossible.[3]

This public and social ideal represented progress in the consciousness of freedom on the part of the human spirit. Freedom to the Greek meant the exact opposite of individual caprice; it was not freedom from something, but consisted rather in acting in accordance with something. To be unfree was to be subject to the unpredictable will of an individual. Freedom lay in the rule of law, in the time-tested wisdom of the sages, preserved and administered by the many.

Hegel was not disposed to overlook the weaknesses of the Greek city-state. He did not forget that slavery existed in Athens, and that slave labor made it possible for citizens to attend to public duties. Nor did he miss the significance of the diminutive size of the city-state and the corresponding homogeneity of interest. These factors had conditioned the rise and development of the kind of democracy the Greeks enjoyed, and made imitation in the modern world foolish, even impossible. But with all its limitations this polity produced in Athens a kind of "vital equality" that stimulated the development of individual talents, and fostered diversity of character and attainment, to an extent unique in history.

Students of antiquity are all impressed with the tragic brevity of Athenian happiness and fortune. The fourth century is a period of steady decline and final ruin. Within one generation the great epoch was irretrievably gone. Philosophers and historians have advanced many explanations of this downfall. Rostovtzeff, an important interpreter of cultural changes, blames the extreme democracy of Athens, and readers of the history of Thucydides can see the truth in this claim. From the perspective of his own time Hegel was certain that the explanation was to be found in a new ethical principle, which acted as a catalyst on the established faith. He would have agreed with Rostovtzeff that Athens went to ruin because of her democratic system, but he would have insisted further that the democracy, so effective in the fifth century, was undermined by the pressure of a new conception of the individual. In a word, fourth century Athens stood under the individualistic sign of the modern world, and the principle of morality (Moralität) came as a presage of ruin to the harmonious, unreflective social ethic.

Seen in terms of Hegel's philosophy of history, the opposition between the fifth and fourth century Athenian ideals is to be understood as an advance from the level of immediate experience, whether in art or religion, to that of reflection. To the customary national ethos of the Periclean age the Ionian-Athenian philosophy had come as a principle of criticism, as an assertion of individual right to examine tradition. The "individuality of beauty" (schöne Individualität), which was an aesthetic union of man and society, was destroyed by the individuality born of reflection. Before the scrutiny of reason the natural and artistic authority could not stand. Hegel recognized critical thought as having the power to destroy before it rebuilds, to criticize before it accepts, to choose before it acts. The Greek Enlightenment, begun by the Sophists and culminating in Socrates, split asunder, as Hegel believed, the immediate and unreflective harmony of the ideal and real world, and plunged Greek civilization into ruin. It prepared the way for what he called *das unglückliche Bewusstsein*, the painful rupture in the soul which prepared the way for the initial acceptance of Christian faith.

For the present purpose it is only necessary to review enough of Hegel's dialectical interpretation of history to illustrate the implications of his contrast of the Greek with the modern Christian world. We have already noticed the emphasis which he placed on training in developing the ethically conscious individual. Education made it possible for man to become aware of what he had hitherto taken for granted, to come to self-consciousness in the principles upon which life and action in society are based. Hegel constantly associated education with morality understood as the sphere of individual conviction and the realm of conscience. In isolation, however, that sphere is the antithesis of a higher social ethic. The individual—such is Hegel's doctrine—must go beyond subjective moral con-

CAMROSE LUTHERAN COLLEGE
LIBRARY

viction and recognize the universal claims of the objective social whole. Individual training and individual conviction alone serve only to separate him from organized society; their influence is negative and destructive. But by means of the separation and pain involved in this subjective attitude man can come to a chastened reconciliation with his world; he can be reborn into a "second nature". Education in this role was for Hegel part of the essential character of modern society.

The Greeks of the fifth century had been without individual discipline; their harmony had been natural. The poets and rhapsodists had been their teachers, but instead of serving as teachers in the modern sense they had fulfilled the function of seers. With the rise of the Sophists the Athenians underwent their first training in the sense of individual intellectual discipline. It was this transition from the poet or seer to the teacher that foreshadowed for Hegel the tragedy of Greece. The Sophists marked the shift, however gradual, from the objective to the subjective, from social to individual standards. It was through them that the Athenians became acquainted with many different ways of regarding things, and became conscious of the need for personal satisfaction in questions of the right and true. The principle of *Nous*, which Anaxagoras had propounded, Hegel found vastly significant in reference to this change. *Nous* was taken by the Sophists in a subjective sense; from it they derived their doctrine that man was the measure of all things. Under the sway of religious, political and poetical ideals the Athenians had not decided questions of right and wrong from subjective conviction, but by reference to the public laws and public oracles. With the advent of education in the form of dialectical and rhetorical proficiency they found that the good and the bad they had hitherto considered sufficiently certain were rendered doubtful. At this point individual conviction began to assert its right over the authority of tradition and objective law.

Such is the picture which Hegel draws at length of the place of education and critical reflection in disrupting the Greek synthesis. It was not merely the particular kind of education made available by the Sophists, but the very fact of education itself. He did not agree with the historical critics who meted out unqualified condemnation upon these teachers of Greece. The Sophists had, to be sure, known well how to make the worse appear the better cause, but, as Hegel remarks in one place, it is always the temptation of the educated man to find a reason for everything. He believed that the educational theory of the Sophists was characteristic of a certain stage in the life of every people. The Greeks impressed Hegel as young, and he sensed that youth in the Sophists' zest for intellectual combat. They were thrilled with the possibilities of many points of view.

They were lured to wider horizons than their people had known. Released from constricting bonds of ancestral and traditional piety, they dared to be intellectual radicals. And Hegel, like other men of his generation, could not but be impressed with the example of these earlier questioners of the established and the accepted.

Now the figure of Socrates appears, "perhaps the most interesting in the philosophy of antiquity", and in Hegel's view one of the most fateful figures in the record of the past. He stands at the parting of the ways and, Janus-faced, looks backwards and before. His character and opinions, set forth in the lectures on the *Philosophy of History* and the *History of Philosophy*, reveal also the double nature of Hegel's own sympathies: the struggle between his classical leanings and the impact of Christian thought, resulting in a kind of double emphasis which, however, cannot be regarded as complete antithesis.

In spite of this doubleness, Hegel presents Socrates as a unified personality, worthy to stand with Pericles, Sophocles, and others whom Hegel so much admired. This is the Socrates of the *Crito*, the philosopher whose piety and veneration for the laws of Athens allowed no personal sense of innocence to supervene, whose radical questions at the same time mark a turning point in the ethical development of mankind. In Socrates Hegel saw the coming to birth of a higher esteem for the individual man, even a precursor of Christ's insight into the worth of human personality. This is the advance in ethical consciousness from intuition or art to thought, from non-rational reliance on custom to rational discrimination. In his sharp opposition to modern rationalistic motivation, Hegel was inclined at times to prefer the aesthetic *Sittlichkeit*. This accounts for a certain ambiguity in his evaluation of Socrates and the Hellenic social ethos in general. His true desire, as will become clear, was to have both, to synthesize the rational determination of ethical values with obedience to the sway of concrete custom and national law. Either of these in isolation led to unbalance and moral error.

"Socrates", wrote Hegel, "is celebrated as a teacher of morality, but we should rather call him the inventor of morality." Before him the Athenians were *sittlich*: they obeyed the customary, and derived their ethical life from the ordinances and usages of the *polis*; after him the rupture with existent reality was complete. In him there first appeared the tendency to question the old virtue; he perceived that it had become doubtful. Filled with this consciousness he tried to establish a new principle of conduct, whose standard was man's intellect. Socrates had eaten the fruit of the tree of knowledge and had become like a god. He derived virtue not from the objective and existent, but from the inner and the intellectual. He had understood Anaxagoras' discovery of *Nous* as the ruler of all, and adopted the Sophists' maxim of man as the measure of all things. But it was man as thinker and as philosopher that was the measure, not man the creature of desire. Thought had become emancipated and the individual as thinker asserted his claim to be judge of his own action.

> We now see Socrates bringing forward the opinion that in these times everyone has to look after his own morality, and thus he looked after his through consciousness and reflection regarding himself; for he sought the universal spirit which had disappeared from reality in his own consciousness.[4]

Socrates found a new and higher freedom than the ethic of beauty could offer; he had arrived at awareness of freedom as intellectual insight and self-determination.

That, in brief, is Hegel's conception of the role of Socrates in ethical history. Even more significant for our purpose is his criticism of Socrates' doctrine. Socrates foreshadowed the accepted principle of the modern world, and for that very reason he was not without the one-sidedness and inadequacy of *Moralität*. The people of Athens brought him to trial and found him guilty of impiety and of corrupting the youth. But he was no martyr. Hegel had only scorn for the ocean of sympathy that posterity had poured over the abrupt end of Socrates' career. His fate was tragedy, it was perhaps the supreme example of ancient tragedy, but it was not martyrdom, since the martyr goes to his death innocent of doing wrong. Twenty pages of the *History of Philosophy* are devoted to the trial and condemnation of Socrates, and most of them are a brief for his accusers. Hegel's reason for this is the fact that Socrates, through his higher ethical apprehension, had brought into question the ancient *Sittlichkeit*. Hence the people were within their right in condemning him.[5]

Hegel criticized the Socratic thesis that virtue was solely the intellectual perception of the good. According to Socrates, virtue consisted in the determination of universal principles and action in accordance with universal, not particular, ends. In this idea of the ethical, Socrates approached what Hegel believed to be the Kantian error of attempting to determine the good as an intellectual and universal form of lawfulness, apart from the particular and the sensuous, and the claims of concrete custom. Here Hegel brings against Socrates the judgment of Aristotle. Aristotle had said of Socrates that he tried to make ethics into a science, by placing all the virtues in the thinking side of the soul and disregarding inclinations and habits. The true conception of morality was for Aristotle more a matter of acquired habit, in which the sympathies and natural impulses receive justification and satisfaction. While knowledge is an essential part, it is not the whole constitution of the good. From the standpoint of his own ethical theory, Hegel wanted to make exactly the same emphasis. As the ethical judgment of Antigone had been one-sided in recognizing as valid only the religious and the traditional, so the Socratic ethic was one-sided in recognizing only the intellectual and the universal. The absolute ethic must include man's alogical as well as his intellectual self. It must be built on the basis of his sensuous necessities, but crowned with the recognition of his spiritual nature.

The refusal of Socrates after his conviction to acknowledge himself in the wrong, while revealing his moral greatness, was proof for Hegel of his disloyalty to the ancient faith. Socrates would not bow before the people. Hegel contrasts him with "the heavenly Antigone", going submissively to her death with the words, "If this seems good unto the gods, suffering, I may be made to know my error." Hegel draws another contrast, this time with the great figure of Pericles who, even as ruler, submitted to the sovereign people and begged them for the life of his friends. He concludes:

> There is nothing dishonoring to the individual in this, for he must bend before the general power, and the real and noblest power is the people. . . . In a general way (Socrates) certainly recognized the sovereignty of the people, but not in this individual case; it has, however, to be recognized, not only in general, but in each separate case.[6]

After briefly considering Hegel's criticism of Plato's *Republic*, we shall be in a position to sum up his interpretation of the Greek social ethos and to understand the contrast with the Kantian *Moralität*. Any one who has become acquainted with Hegel's theory of the state will be aware of the great influence which Plato's masterpiece had exercised upon him. It is not my purpose to dwell upon this relationship.[7] But it is important to know that Hegel considered the *Republic* to be an attempt at reconstruction of the fifth century ethic of custom. Aware of the new subjective principle and its work of destruction, Plato tried to build up a theory of the state that would make the individual citizens entirely dependent upon an objective order. This should not imply that Plato himself had not advanced beyond the aesthetic and unreflective morality embodied in Antigone. He had fully recognized Socrates' discovery, but he desired a return on the rational level of that which had exercised implicit control in the older *Sittlichkeit*. Though Hegel conceded that Plato, aware of the harmful forces at work, had gone further in the exclusion of individualism than a fifth century Athenian would have done, he was nevertheless convinced that the *Republic* represented the true spirit of the Periclean Age.

The supreme worth of Plato's ethical philosophy, according to Hegel, lay in its recognition that in objective institutions, in the state and its concrete laws, was to be found the nature of justice and all the moral virtues. Only in the concrete realization of the highest individual desires in such an organization can there be any ethical life and action worthy of the name. The fiction of a state of nature positing the idea of the individual's free will in relationship to others—this evil modern delusion—was not admitted by the author of the *Republic*. For him the greatest freedom was the greatest communal life.

> Plato . . . lays as his foundation the substantial, the universal, and he does this in such a way that the individual as such has this very universal as his end, and the subject has his will, activity, life and enjoyment in the state, so that it may be called his second nature, his habits and his customs. This moral substance which constitutes the spirit, life and being of individuality, and which is its foundation, systematizes itself into a living organic whole, and at the same time differentiates itself into its members, whose activity signifies the production of the whole.[8]

Impressed as Hegel was by this Platonic notion of the organic relation of individual and society, and the dependence of the part on the whole, he was, nevertheless, convinced of the presence of a great defect.

> Plato in his *Republic* represents the substantive ethical life in its ideal beauty and truth. But with the principle of independent particularity, which broke in upon Greek ethical life at his time, he could do nothing except to oppose it to his Republic, which is simply substantive. Hence he excluded even the earliest form of subjectivity, as it exists in private property and the family, and also in its more expanded form as private liberty and choice of profession. . . . In the merely substantive form of the actual spirit, as it appears in Plato, the principle of self-dependent and in itself infinite personality of the individual, the principle of subjective freedom does not receive its due.[9] . . .
>
> In the Platonic state subjective freedom has not as yet any place, since in it the rulers assigned to individuals their occupations. . . . But subjective freedom, which must be respected, demands free choice for individuals.[10]

This absence of subjective freedom represented the basic defect in the Hellenic social ethos.

The important difference between the ideal modern ethics and Greek ethics lay for Hegel in the principle of insight into the nature of right. In his *Philosophy of Right*, he distinguishes between an act performed from habituation and custom and one performed from a clear conviction of its truth and rightness. Socrates made the same distinction though he was unable to see the other elements in morality. Hegel did not condemn Socrates' insight, only his one-sidedness. Nor did he—at least in theory— oppose the basic assumption of Kantian morality, which to him seemed closely allied with the Socratic doctrine. In a little essay, entitled *Was heiszt Aufklärung*, Kant maintained that Enlightenment signified primarily the right of the individual to make his own moral decisions. That would include freedom from the unreasoned authority imposed by hereditary monarchs. Though Hegel remained rebellious to the idea of a moral imperative arising out of an independent principle of conscience, he affirmed this cardinal doctrine of the individual's right to insight into the principles upon which he acts and satisfaction with them. His quarrel with the Kantian concept of duty was, as has been said, the fact that it was conceived as a pure rational imperative, divorced from and opposed to impulses, habits and instincts, and had become a bare abstraction, incapable of initiating any action at all. Duty or conscience, however, conceived as the rational content of past social experience, awareness of the ideal rationality of individual life in the perspective of the whole, was for Hegel concrete, vital, and indeed the only spring of moral action. Hence his theory of an absolute *Sittlichkeit* was an effort to transcend the individualist conception of morality, not by disregarding it, but by bringing about a synthesis between this kind of *Moralität* and the Greek social and objective ethos. The individual, in this view, must first attain to the "moral" standpoint through a process of education and intellectual discipline, before he can become reconciled with objective laws and attain the higher social ethic.

Hegel approved wholeheartedly Plato's emphasis in the *Republic* on social and political organization, and the priority given to the community over the individual. But he profoundly disagreed with the assumption that the reasoning element is limited to the philosopher-kings, that it is a property of rulers and not of the ruled. In Hegel's ideal state all the citizens were in this respect to be on a level with the Platonic rulers. The virtue of the ruled in Plato's state was only submission to rule, whereas Hegel conceived of obedience as insight into the rational nature of the relationship between the subject and authority. Freedom was for Hegel compatible with obedience, a conception which Plato had not been able to allow or perhaps to understand.[11]

M. P. Foster in his book on *The Political Philosophies of Plato and Hegel* points out the crux of the difference between the principle of law (Themis), which guided Hegel, and the principle of custom (Nomos), which forms the basis of ethos in the *Republic*. Law as a product of conscious thought implies rational mediation on the part of the person who is subject to it. Custom, as the product of inheritance and accepted sentiment, requires no such mediation. Custom can operate without the subject's awareness, it can determine his action down to the minutest detail. In its very nature custom is concrete and particular, whereas law is general and requires individual judgment for its particular application. While this distinction of Foster's is relevant in relation to the *Republic*, he pushes it too far when he generalizes Plato's conception of ruler and ruled to apply to the whole of Greek political theory, and when he maintains that the Greeks never realized the difference between the ruled as a subject and as an instrument or tool. For him the development of modern political philosophy is based on the recognition, "which the Greeks lacked, that freedom is compatible with obedience to command".[12] Hegel would not have agreed to such a generalization, particularly in the light of his interpretation of Socrates and Aristotle. The difference, however, between custom and law and the widening of individual participation implied in the concept of law are wholly in line with his critique of Plato.

Hegel conceived that this difference really involved a new understanding of freedom in the modern world. To the modern man freedom can exist only when his reason approves as valid the principle upon which he acts. Hegel recognized and sought to grant this primary claim of Kantian morality. That is the meaning of his aphorism that in Greece only "the few" were free, whereas in the Christian world all are, or have the recognized right to be, free. This involved a genuine advance in self-consciousness on the part of the human spirit. Greek *Sittlichkeit*, as a natural and unmediated harmony of particular and universal had been replaced, according to this theory, by a conception involving the rebirth of the individual through conflict with the immediate and natural into the intellectual kingdom. This ethos of second nature was envisaged by Hegel not only as an outgrowth of habit and custom but as containing the element of conscience, the individual right to acquiesce with what the state commands. The Greek had proceeded from an artistic union of the individual and society; the Christian required an intellectual union.

Yet Hegel could not agree with the predominant modern view of the state as essentially an artificial product, resulting from a social contract. Though law for him implied a more self-conscious level of understanding than did custom, he was not prepared to grant that law arose solely out of individual intelligence and creative will. The difference between Greek and modern ethical conceptions lay for him in the difference between what is created and what is discovered. For the Greek philosophers the principles governing state and society were not created by the individual will but already existent in the universe. The state involved for Plato the discovery of rational forms, not their invention. Accordingly the state could be derived from rational principles, because those principles were implicit in the nature of things. The state was therefore natural as social living was natural; it was only the individual in isolation that was unnatural and illogical. With this fundamental conception Hegel heartily agreed. He opposed the whole modern emphasis on the creativity of will as an independent, non-rational activity. Will in his philosophy is subsumed under intellect, and the intellect is governed largely by the capacity to know and understand rather than to create.

Here lies a serious difficulty in Hegel's ethical ideals. In his reaction against the extreme individualism of his people in their political consciousness, he swung too far in the direction of the collective and absolute in ethics. The reader of the *Philosophy of Right* observes with surprise that its author could not conceive of any real situation in which individual and social interests might conflict, and that he recognized no ethical value of genuine worth that was not represented by the state.[13] In the end one can hardly escape the conclusion that Hegel's state would be as unsuited for happiness as Plato's republic.

Whatever the difficulties in his own ethical doctrines, it must be concluded that Hegel's criticism of Greek ethics reveals in particular two things: It shows how deeply his sympathies were involved in his attitude toward the pre-Christian pagan ethos, and how impossible a task he conceived it to be even as a mature thinker to build a positive, social ethic on Christian culture alone. If the classical preferences of his youth were largely carried over into his later evaluation of Greek religion, the same is hardly less true in the moral sphere. Yet the problem here went deeper. It seems to me that Hegel had become thoroughly aware of the deep perplexity of the problem of the relation of the individual and society. He was conscious that there had been no permanently satisfactory solution of this either in ancient or in modern times. He no longer rushed into large and easy generalizations about the Greek ethic. He no longer saw it as a simple, one-fold religious ethos, but as a synthesis of diverse elements, a synthesis, furthermore, that contained definite limitations. Though he held no illusions as to the possibility or desirability of reviving this objective, social ethos, it remained for him the only approach to the solution of the ethical problem. In his critical treatment of Greek philosophy we shall see that the same conviction is even more strikingly evident in the realm of philosophical thought.

V

MINERVA'S OWL

The concept of development is, as we have seen, central in Hegel's philosophy. His vision of the human world as a whole was that of a vast organism developing in history from the potential to the actual, from the implicit to the explicit, from the isolated to the free. Movement, progress, change in general was to be understood in terms of development between these two poles of potentiality and reality. This living structure contained within itself in germ all the content that was to become manifest and revealed. In this particular sense, there was for Hegel nothing new in history, nothing original or accidental. In the unfolding of the world organism, no new content was added that was not already implicit. Yet he felt the difference to be enormous between the potential and the actual, the latent powers and substantial reality. All the variation in the development of human history grew out of this difference. To use his own metaphor, it was the difference between the child and the mature—or perhaps we should rather say, the old—man, between unconscious natural power and conscious ripened wisdom. Progress in history was due to the increasing degree of the actualization of reason and spirit in man and society. Development was from the natural toward the spiritual, from the slavery of blind desire toward the freedom of understanding. Thought was the highest and final level of human development, the spirit's consciousness of the independence of its true nature. The divine life itself was the highest development of pure spirit, the realization of complete self-dependence, the true freedom.

> Everything that from eternity has happened in heaven and earth, the life of God and all the deeds of time simply are the struggles for mind to know itself, and finally unite itself to itself; it is alienated and divided, but only so as to be able thus to find itself and return to itself.[1]

This is the great Hegelian mythology and philosophic vision. It should be so understood and interpreted.

In terms of this conception of organic spiritual development Hegel expounded the history of philosophy. There could be, he taught, no really original philosophy. Progress in the history of thought involved no new beginnings. "We are what we are through history." Every new idea, each new system of thought caught up and reinterpreted what had gone before.

Every age developed its view of the world from the traditions handed down by the past. Yet tradition for Hegel was not a mere housekeeper who preserved the spiritual treasures of the generations. He made use of a different simile and likened the philosophic tradition to "a mighty river, which increases in size the further it advances from its source".[2] Every appropriation of the thought of the past involved superseding it. Goethe had said "that which is formed continually resolves itself back into matter", which meant to Hegel that any form again and again becomes the material for a new and higher form. He was fascinated by the application of this thought to intellectual history. The inheritance of the past constituted the spiritual capital of each new generation. But entering upon the legacy, the new age re-applied it to erect for itself a more adequate spiritual home. In this way the past was preserved within the present, but was changed and enriched by the restless activity of reason.

Every new system of philosophy grasped part of the truth, but none was entirely adequate. One supplemented another and every fresh view reincorporated some former idea in the attempt to avoid one-sidedness and contradiction. Like a spiral, this process wound upwards, each turn complete in itself, but progressively attaining higher levels.[3]

So Hegel conceived of the history of Greek philosophy as an ascending progress in which each new outlook included the truth of all the former points of view within a wider and more adequate horizon. From Thales to Aristotle thought widened from a simple, abstract philosophy of nature through a more refined ethical emphasis, to a complete and rounded philosophy, including the science of logic, philosophy of nature, and philosophy of spirit. There was an uninterrupted transcending of the past until in Aristotle, Greek thought reached its peak. According to Hegel, his work epitomized the Greek contribution to history.

By the time that Greek philosophy reached this peak of complete formulation in Plato and Aristotle, the social and cultural synthesis was passed. The Periclean Age had become history; the break, as Hegel put it, between thought and existent reality was complete. The philosophers had become private men, withdrawn into the world of reflection, idlers in the people's sight. As he looked upon this cultural phenomenon Hegel saw something that was applicable to all great periods of history: namely, that philosophy was always an end-of-the-epoch product. Art and religion belonged to the spirit of a people in its emergence and up to its full bloom. Philosophy came only after happiness and fortune had passed. Like the wisdom of an old man whose physical vigor has waned, it stood helpless before the inexorable tide of history.

Philosophy as the thought of the world, does not appear until reality has completed its formative process, and made itself ready. History thus corroborates the teaching of the conception that only in the maturity of reality does the ideal appear as counterpart to the real, and apprehend the real world in its substance and shape it into an intellectual kingdom. When philosophy paints its grey in grey, one form of life has become old, and by means of grey it cannot be rejuvenated but only known. The owl of Minerva takes its flight only when the shades of night are gathering.[4]

Another consideration basic to Hegel's interpretation of the history of philosophy is inherent in this idea of development, namely the concept of the concrete. Hegel insisted that the true is always the concrete; abstractions are imperfect, even unreal representations of the actual. True thought concerns specific, existent particulars, not as particulars but in connection with their inherent universal relations and structures. The idea of the concrete became for Hegel identified with the concept of dialectic as the method of arriving at truth. Reason perceives the universal and the essential, not in abstracting from particular content, but within the particular content itself. The intelligible structure of things and ideas is to be apprehended not by a method of reductive analysis but by understanding their interrelatedness and their mutual development.

Hegel's great desire was to escape the unresolved contradictions of thought which eighteenth century rationalism and unorganic science had left to posterity. He was convinced that those difficulties arose largely from the analytic method of reasoning, which consisted in the reduction of material to essential components, the process of dividing and isolating in order to understand. This analytic method of the Enlightenment Hegel called *Raisonniren.* He found its most destructive products in the antinomies of Kant's *Critique of Pure Reason,* in which the human intellect is perplexed and defeated by irreconcilable contradictions. These contradictions resulted from failure to conceive the total nature of any specific content in its development and interrelatedness. Analysis, the instrument of understanding (Verstand), breaks up living organic wholes, and attempts to conceive of them apart from their function and development. Synthesis, the instrument of reason (Vernunft), perceives the underlying powers that control the total structure, and proceeds on the assumption that the whole alone is true. Hegel thus equated analysis with unreality because it is the attempt to understand the essential structure of material apart from its context and divorced from the realm of process. He believed that his logic, as a logic of reason (Vernunft), was able to grasp the synthetic course of development, to read history in terms of related, progressive wholes.

Hence in conceiving the concrete, Hegel identified it with his idea of development by dialectical process. The concrete alone is true, and the concrete is movement—it is developing structure. Moreover, the concrete is essentially the union of opposite determinations. In process, in evolvement, things become what they were not; they grow not in linear direction, but between the poles of opposites. The ascent to new levels implied that the previous stages had not been destroyed, but that they were a necessary phase of the process. This method of interpreting the past—what Hegel called "speculative thinking"—was, as we have seen, based on the proposition that contradictions and oppositions in thought as in the empirical world are resolved by movement from one pole to the other. Unity results through the process which is at the same time concrete and universal.

> The concrete is the unity of diverse determinations and principles; these in order to be perfected, in order to come definitely before the consciousness, must first be developed in separation. Thereby they acquire the aspect of one-sidedness in comparison with the higher principle which follows. This, nevertheless, does not annihilate them, nor even leave them where they were, but takes them up into itself as moments.[5]

This idea of the concrete in the history of philosophy meant for Hegel simply the progressive viewing of phenomena in wider and wider contexts; it involved becoming conscious of interrelationships and more far-reaching unities. For him it was not, as has often been the case with others, a process of increasing abstraction, but rather the opposite. The more inclusive became the context, the more concrete and specific became the understanding of the intellectual world. The early philosophers had been aware of comparatively few relations. They conceived of simple principles to explain phenomena. Their concepts had been separate, isolated, partial, and as a result abstract. Hegel believed that as systems of thought advanced in complexity and in the recognition of the interrelatedness of ideas as well as of natural phenomena, they also advanced in concreteness and truth. But for him the concrete was never the particular, the empirical individual, nor was it a single idea. It was the complex of ideas, the union of individuals, the organism in its entirety. As conceived by Hegel in his Logic, the concrete does not really allow for individuation as such; as a logical principle, the individual is inessential and lacks reality. The failure to do justice to the empirical particular has long been recognized as a cardinal weakness of his point of view.[6]

Seen in this light, the concrete as characterizing the advance in Greek philosophy meant growth in completeness and inclusiveness of philosophical systems; it meant advance from simple and unrelated ideas to the complex and the contextual. Hegel traced this advance in terms of schools of thought. Greek philosophy had gone through several stages in its progress to concrete determinations. There had been, first, the abstract speculations of the early Ionian schools; these had been followed by the Pythagorean and Eleatic numerical abstractions and the idea of the oneness of being. The Sophists and Socrates formed a second period in which thought abandoned natural speculations and turned inward to ethical questions, but still remained abstract in so far as it attempted to determine the good apart from content. Only in Plato and Aristotle had Greek philosophy realized the full truth of the concrete in Hegel's sense, and of the two Aristotle had advanced farthest in concreteness. In evaluating the Hellenistic schools, Stoic, Epicurean, Sceptic, according to this theory, Hegel denied that they were really Greek, maintaining that in spirit they belonged to the Roman world whose very nature was abstractness. Only at the very end of the Roman period had the Alexandrian philosophy, by a return to Plato and Aristotle, partially overcome the abstractions of the Hellenistic period and grasped the real in its concrete determinations, as the unity of God and the world in the concept of the Trinity.[7]

From these two related Hegelian ideas of development and the concrete, we can now turn to a closer examination of the parts of Hegel's history of philosophy which are especially relevant to our purpose. The reader's first impression on taking up the three volumes of lectures in Glockner's edition is that a disproportionate space is devoted to the consideration of Greek thought. Of the 1,700 pages, one hundred and eighty are given to the Introduction and a brief sketch of Oriental thought, and over nine hundred and fifty are concerned with the Greeks. Only five hundred pages are left for the treatment of European thought through the Middle Ages to Schelling. When one has gone through these volumes the first impression is confirmed: that the history of philosophy was for Hegel preeminently the history of Greek thought. Among the moderns only Leibniz and Spinoza receive what could be considered adequate attention.

In Hegel's treatment of the Greek philosophers the reader is constantly impressed by the thoroughness of his knowledge and the keenness of his interest. Here he was most completely at home. He devoted years to the preparation of these studies and reworked them again and again till they became the most adequate of all his lectures. They reveal his painstaking care and the intense devotion of his philosophic spirit. When once a student has gone through them carefully he is no longer in doubt as to where to begin the study of Hegel, for they are the best introduction to his whole philosophy.

This does not mean that his treatment of Greek philosophy is without errors and serious defects. Though Hegel dealt with the original sources to a greater extent than most scholars before him, subsequent research has revealed errors in detail as well as in larger issues. An obvious illustration is his somewhat uncritical use of secondary Greek and Latin sources for the pre-Socratic philosophers. For example, Hegel consulted Diogenes Laertius, Sextus Empiricus, to a less extent Simplicius, and above all, Aristotle's historical references, in an attempt to fill out the fragmentary picture of the lives and opinions of the Greek thinkers. Modern scholarship has questioned these sources with good reason. Hegel particularly relied on Aristotle's opinions of his predecessors and contemporaries and championed those opinions at the expense of all conflicting evidence. Yet these statements of Aristotle on historical subjects are regarded with particular suspicion by scholars today.

Because Hegel himself relied on the original works and insisted on the need for historical objectivity he directs the full force of his harsh polemic against the then current histories of J. J. Brucker and Wilhelm Tennemann, the former a historian of the school of Christian Wolff, the latter a disciple of Kant. He found them both flagrantly guilty of reading modern ideas into ancient systems of thought. Yet it seems to me obvious that in spite of his consciousness of the problem, Hegel himself was not wholly free from the faults of which he accused his predecessors. Though on the whole he was governed by what was explicitly contained in the sources before him, his philosophical presuppositions sometimes led to implications hard to justify on the basis of the works themselves. This is particularly true in his interpretations of thinkers with whom he felt spiritual affinity. One example of his lack of historical caution occurs in his treatment of Heraclitus, that mysterious figure of antiquity, whom he regarded as a forefather of his own logical system. His interpretation of the scanty Heraclitan remains is thought-provoking, but not critical enough to meet the modern standard.

It may be well to mention here the more general source of Hegel's misinterpretations of Greek philosophy. This was his passion for logic. Hegel believed that the dialectical method had been discovered and developed in Greece, and his tracing of that development caused him to neglect and sometimes to misinterpret non-logical values. Moreover, the attempt to apply his own logical structure to the understanding of the course of Greek thought is responsible for most of the false theories so often lashed by critics. This passion for logic led Hegel to the impossible assumption that the historical order of appearance of the systems of philosophy was the same as the necessary succession of ideas in terms of his own logic. He tried to assert that everything in the history of philosophy was a necessary and consequent progress according to logical schemata, each thinker providing a level in the unfolding of an inevitable logical pattern. This notion, which appears as early as the *Phenomenology of Spirit*, has been condemned· too often to need further remark. If the modern student is to appreciate the positive insights of Hegel into Greek philosophy, as in other areas of his thought, it is necessary to pass over this personal idiosyncrasy and to seek to penetrate the more objective critical recesses of his historical judgments.

On the other hand, we can hardly quarrel with Hegel for selecting those ideas in Greek philosophy which appealed to him as most significant. He was no friend of the type of historicism that insists that a critic have no point of view of his own and attempt to judge the past dispassionately and objectively. When Hegel devoted special attention to the two concepts of dialectic and *Nous* or reason, he was stressing two major motifs of his own thought, which he found to have been discovered and partially elaborated by the pre-Socratics. The Eleatics (especially Zeno) and Heraclitus concerned him most in the development of dialectic; Anaxagoras, the Sophists, and later Socrates in the discovery of the principle of *Nous*. Other philosophers to whom other ideas appeared central have chosen to emphasize other thinkers among the early Greeks.

In Parmenides and Zeno, Hegel saw the beginning of real· philosophy. In them thought had become emancipated from identification with the Ionic school's emphasis on nature as well as from the Pythagorean cult of numbers. It began to reflect on its own nature, to think in terms of concepts (*Begriffe*), rather than in physical and objective terms. The Eleatics, Hegel asserts, were the first philosophers because they were the first speculative, the first dialectical thinkers.

Hegel was at pains to distinguish two important kinds of dialectic in his treatment of the pre-Socratics: the subjective or negative and the objective or positive dialectic. Only the subjective was really known to the Eleatics, and in it Zeno had made himself the unsurpassed master. Hegel's distinction between the two is important. The immanent movement of thought divorced from objective considerations, is characteristic of the subjective dialectic. It attempts by means of reasoning to render the evidence of the senses contradictory, that is, to establish a universal proposition by refuting particular instances. The objective or higher dialectic, to which Hegel was especially devoted and which he believed Heraclitus had discovered, he defined not as the outward activity of subjective thinking, but as the movement within the soul of the content of thought itself. "We term dialectic", he wrote in the *Science of Logic,* "that higher movement of reason where terms appearing absolutely distinct pass into one another because they are what they are, where the assumption of their separateness cancels itself."[8] Both kinds Hegel distinguished from the "external dialectic" characteristic of eighteenth-century rationalism or *Verstandesraisonniren,* which developed the conflicting sides of some general principle and arrived at unresolved antinomies. The consequence of such dialectic led to the conclusion that human knowledge is only appearance and not the real world. Such subjectivity of thought and consequent dualism of reason and being Hegel correctly insisted was unknown to the Greeks.[9]

But he found the subjective dialectic in its Eleatic form valuable only as an instrument of criticism and destruction. The Sophists mastered it and used it to make what was formerly secure seem uncertain and to dissolve the particular by reference to the universal. Hegel admired this intellectual skill, and felt, as did Aristotle, that it had real significance. But he knew that as an instrument it was powerless to promote an understanding of the world. For example, Parmenides had conceived of the truth as a single undifferentiated unity, and Zeno had bent the whole energy of his dialectic to the establishment of the same questionable principle by making both change and movement logically absurd.

From Hegel's point of view the Eleatics with their subjective dialectic and their abstract principle of being yielded in interest to the striking figure of Heraclitus. He had achieved greater concreteness in defining his principle of truth, not as being, but as becoming. He had developed dialectic not merely as the movement of subjective thought, but also as the rhythm of the objective world. In Heraclitus' famous phrases, "all things flow, nothing endures", "being and non-being are the same; everything is and yet it is not", Hegel found a truth which had influenced Plato and Aristotle and had endured even to his own day. Hegel believed that Heraclitus had reduced the static world of Parmenides to the fluid world of change, that he had rendered objective what, except for occasional hints, had remained subjective in Zeno. He recognized that being and non-being are abstractions devoid of final meaning, and that the first truth is to be found in becoming. Heraclitus, in Hegel's opinion, made the great discovery that any principle seen in isolation and at rest is illusion and the very soul of untruth. Zeno had asserted the proposition that from nothing comes nothing, but Heraclitus' insight advanced to the realization that in the flow of all things opposites combine to form a unity, to make a life. Truth as movement thus became the union of the subjective and objective, of content and form. In this concept of objective dialectic as the resolution of the abstractions of being and non-being in the idea of becoming, we have the essential basis of Hegel's system. However far Heraclitus was from conceiving this developed idea—and I believe the Hegelian interpretation goes far beyond the implications of such Heraclitan fragments as we possess—it is unquestionable that this early Greek philosopher played a suggestive role in Hegel's development. He concluded his critical treatment of this subject with the comment: "There is no proposition of Heraclitus which I have not adopted in my Logic."[10]

But we may detect on further reading that this advance was not so great as might at first appear. Change in itself without something which abides and maintains itself through change is without final meaning. The concept which Hegel considered central in Greek philosophy was Aristotle's basic idea of natural teleology, in which change becomes process and progress toward an end implicit in the organism that undergoes the change. And he applied this principle, much as Aristotle himself had done, to judge the early thinkers. Heraclitus had conceived of change only, not of direction or purposiveness, not of the sense of realization and fulfilment of an immanent potentiality. According to Hegel, change itself must have pattern and structure, and it was in this failure to determine the true nature of becoming that Heraclitus failed in concreteness and truth.

Hegel applied the same essential criticism to the principle of Anaxagoras, the concept of *Nous* or reason. This was the second great discovery of philosophy and in a manner it supplied what had been wanting in Heraclitus. The principle of *Nous*, if Anaxagoras had conceived of it aright, signified just this idea of purposiveness in nature and man: it meant law, direction, process as universal reason. But for Anaxagoras, though he sought to understand *Nous* as the simple principle and essence of things, it remained formal and inapplicable to the natural world of human society. Hegel repeated and emphasized Plato's criticism in the *Phaedo* concerning the abstract nature of Anaxagoras' doctrine. He had not conceived of reason otherwise than as a universal form, nor had he applied it to determinate and concrete activity. Only Aristotle, as Hegel believed, had properly estimated reason as the origin and structure of the objective world and at the same time recognized its subjective application to a determinate process. Anaxagoras conceived of reason as static form, Aristotle, as purposive, universal, yet particular activity. It was he who had bridged the chasm between particular and universal, between form and content, subjective and objective by his insight into the nature of reason as activity, as teleological self-realization.

Thus Hegel found in the principles of Heraclitus and Anaxagoras two of the main constituents of his own philosophy. But the bare conception of these principles by the early Greeks was far from suggesting their concrete determination and the true realization of the relations between them. Hegel, unlike many German historians who were to follow him, did not set too high a value on the contributions of the pre-Socratics. He knew that the originality and greatness of a thinker lay more in the use and application of the materials at hand than in the discovery of new and isolated truths. These early philosophers had after all, he concluded, accomplished little—except to furnish material and a tradition for the greater thinkers who were to come after them. Their efforts had not been lost; the future had preserved and expanded their meanings. Only in the light of later developments did these first attempts take on real significance.

With this we come to the heart of the matter, to Hegel's understanding of Plato and Aristotle. In the first place his vigorous quarrel with the traditions that had grown up around these two great thinkers determined to a great extent his critical treatment. Tradition, especially modern habits of interpretation[11], had separated them and had made Plato "the patron saint of mere enthusiasm" and Aristotle the progenitor of empiricism in philosophy. Plato was the fountain head of all idealism, Aristotle the source of realism; Plato had originated the idea, the ideal and the transcendent, Aristotle had explored the real and the empirical. Plato had been the speculative thinker, Aristotle the sober scientist and research scholar. Hegel, approaching their thought at first hand in the Greek, was convinced that tradition had been unjust to both. It was true that some reason could be found in their works for most of the opinions in the centuries which followed, but it was equally true that the *Epigonen* had been blind to what Plato and Aristotle really taught. They had missed the total impression of their philosophies and had fastened upon isolated aspects. For Hegel the difference between Aristotelian realism and Platonic idealism— in so far as he admitted a difference at all—was superficial and non-essential. Platonic idealism implied for him nothing of the transcendent or otherworldly, and Aristotelian realism denied none of the speculative reaches of the intellect. Aristotle completed Plato and gave concrete and purified expression to what he had left abstract and mythical. Plato had opened the intellectual world through insistence on the reality of universals; Aristotle gave that world concrete realization in his conception of organic purposiveness.

With Plato, Hegel's sense of the injustice of tradition coupled with his own strong interests led him partly in the right direction and partly astray. Hegel felt that the basic source of the misinterpretation of Plato lay in a failure to separate the content from the manner of presentation. Plato had couched his thought in poetic dialogues, and though Hegel could himself appreciate the value and charm of this manner of presentation, he found Plato's meaning more often concealed than revealed, at least to an unimaginative posterity. Plato lacked systematic form, and his philosophy had to be extracted from artistic metaphor and pleasing externalities.

His philosophy is not, properly speaking, presented there in systematic form, and to construct it from such writings is difficult, not so much from anything in itself, as because this philosophy has been differently understood in different times; and more than all, because it has been much and roughly handled in modern times by those who have either read into it their own crude notions, being unable to conceive the spiritual spiritually, or have regarded as the essential and most significant element in Plato's philosophy that which in reality does not belong to philosophy at all, but only to the mode of presentation.[12]

With real justice and insight, Hegel ridiculed the moderns who had taken too literally the Platonic metaphors and the images concerning the separation of the soul into rational and irrational elements in the famous *Phaedrus* myth, the idea of knowledge as recollection, implying a previous existence in the *Meno*, and the myth of the creation of the world in the *Timaeus*. These and other similar Platonic "doctrines" Hegel insisted belonged only to the mode of presentation. They were poetic metaphors never meant to be interpreted literally. This was Plato's way of giving popular and figurative form to philosophic truth. But posterity had fastened on the external and non-essential and had made it the very essence of his thought. Hegel attributed this habit of taking Plato literally, this unimaginative dogmatizing of his poetic expression, not to too much acquaintance with philosophy on the part of modern readers but to too little. "In truth, it is only ignorance of philosophy that renders it difficult to grasp the philosophy of Plato."[13]

However, in his quarrel with tradition Hegel certainly went too far in separating Platonic content from Platonic form. He could not realize that Plato was artist as well as philosopher, and that the separation could never be complete. Hegel's absorption with logic prevented him from doing justice to the poetic insights of Plato. He objected to the Platonic language on the ground that it prevented its author from expressing himself in conceptual form. Impelled to understand the metaphysical and logical essence of this philosophy, he brushed aside the form in which it was cast, and which many of us today regard as an inseparable part of the substance. Everything poetic, even the myths in which Plato tried to express the truths that eluded logical form, Hegel set down to Plato's inadequacy, an inadequacy which was overcome in Aristotle's sober, conceptual mode of expression. "The myth", he says, "belongs to the pedagogic stage (Pädogogie) of the human race. When the concept has developed, it no longer needs the myth."[14]

Hegel dismissed roughly and unjustly Schleiermacher's attempts to interpret the meaning of Plato as artist-philosopher. He was also out of sympathy with Schleiermacher's textual criticism and his efforts to determine the authenticity of certain dialogues.

It is quite superfluous for philosophy, and belongs to the hyper-criticism of our times, to treat Plato from a literary point of view, critically examining whether one or another of the minor dialogues is genuine or not. Regarding the more important of the dialogues, we may mention that the testimony of the ancients themselves leaves not the slightest doubt.[15]

What was it, then, that Plato had accomplished in the history of philosophy that rendered his thought so epoch-making? Hegel answered in effect that the contribution of Plato was his conception that the true is the universal, and that the way to that truth is not through the senses, but through thought. Plato opened the kingdom of the intellect, and was the first fully to grasp the fact that the rational, that is, the spiritual, was the very essence of the universe. In this he had followed and extended the doctrine of his teacher, Socrates, who had maintained the absolute right of self-conscious thought. Plato, however, had given it objective existence and rendered it applicable in a way that Socrates had been unable to do. Socrates had advanced beyond the arbitrariness and subjectivity of the Sophists' doctrine of reason and had discovered the principle that the content of *Nous* was the universally true and right and good. His tragedy came about for the reason described in the previous chapter, that he had not found the true relation of universals to particular existence. In Hegel's view, Plato rendered objective and concrete Socrates' great doctrine of the reality and truth of self-aware reason. He had subtracted from it all subjective character and conceived it as the unified structure of the intelligible world.

Hegel perceived in Plato passion for knowledge, emphasis on the theoretical, and love of wisdom. He was the thinker who had made for philosophy the highest claims ever conceived. What attracted the German philosopher was the intrinsic connection he saw in the Greek between the real and the ideal, the soul and the body. Hegel thrust aside the long tradition of Platonic dualism. For him Plato unified the objective and the subjective, the divine and the human by discovering that they are parts of the same reality. This was the monism that Hegel desired and believed that he had found in the author of the dialogues.[16]

For Hegel this was the significance of the so-called "theory of ideas". Modern thinkers had conceived them either as aesthetic ideals within the mind of man, to be immediately appropriated by intuition, or as the kind of substance which lay beyond and outside the individual in a transcendent realm. Against these views Hegel advanced the interpretation of the ideas as universals, brought forth and realized through the process of conceptual knowledge. As such they were neither irrational poetic ideals nor independent entities. According to Hegel, Plato was endeavoring to express the truth that the particulars which are first in consciousness are not the basically real, but that the universal forms, the species, the genus, the class, of which the particular is only a representative, remain the ultimate. In this Hegel acknowledged that Plato had been a supreme teacher of the human race. He summed up Plato's teaching in the exhortation to seek truth in the intellectual world, in that conceptual knowledge whose very nature is the character of universals.

Plato had apprehended by means of dialectic that only the universal is true and for Hegel this Platonic dialectic itself proved to be an element of supreme value in his philosophy. Among the preceding philosophies Hegel distinguished between two kinds of dialectic, the subjective, sophistic type, the chief intention of which was to confuse and destroy, and the speculative type the reality of which lay in insight into the unity of contradictions. Plato had used and extended both kinds. Hegel believed that the purpose of many of the dialogues was the negative one of confounding men with contradictions within the realm of the particular and the sensuous, in order to convince them of the existence of a science of universals. Plato had shown that there are not many virtues but that virtue is one, not many kinds of beauty but a universal form of beauty. This dialectic Plato had learned from its originator, Zeno, and from the Sophists who knew so well how to disintegrate the particular.

But Hegel felt that Plato had gone further than that. He had found the way to preserve the individual in the universal, to unify and bring together the real world and the ideal world, a union effected by means of objective dialectic. The German philosopher turned to the later dialogues, the *Sophist*, *Philebus* and, especially, *Parmenides*, to establish his claim that Plato had conceived the whole substance of the speculative philosophy. In *Parmenides*, "the masterpiece of Platonic dialectic", Hegel found the truth revealed of the unity of being and non-being in the concept of realization or end. "Plato first comprehended the Absolute as the Being of *Parmenides*, but as the universal which as species, is also end, i.e. which rules, penetrates, and produces the particular and manifold."[17] Here Plato had reached the great affirmative truth that the contradictions between the many particulars and the one universal are overcome in the movement of knowledge. This union of what is different, of the one and the many, of being and non-being, was not effected by mere juxtaposition or transition from one to the other, but by the recognition of the presence of the one in the other. Non-being was held to be a constituent part of being, as the many were implicit in the one. The very nature of things and ideas consisted in this union of opposites. As Hegel sums up his conclusions drawn from the *Parmenides*, he states what amounts to the substance of his whole logic.

> Freedom exists only in a return into itself; the undifferentiated is the lifeless; the active living, concrete universal is hence what inwardly differentiates itself, but yet remains free in so doing. Now this determinateness consists in the one being identical with itself in the other, in the many, in what is differentiated. This constitutes the only truth and the only interest for knowledge in what is called Platonic philosophy, and if this is not known, the main point of it is not known.[18]

Many have disputed Hegel's claim that the substance of his objective dialectic is to be found in the later dialogues of Plato. Ernst Bratuscheck,[19] one of Hegel's more violent opponents in the nineteenth century, maintained that Hegel's translation of certain passages in the *Parmenides* was inaccurate and that his interpretation of others was more inaccurate still. His final conclusion was that the dialogue itself was spurious, and for that reason, if for no other, Hegel's whole conception of Plato was false. Bratuscheck's attack is extreme but it is beyond my purpose to investigate this intricate problem. Scholars have never agreed as to what Plato really implied in this difficult dialogue. But it can hardly be doubted that Hegel found in the *Parmenides*, and to a less extent in the *Sophist* and *Philebus*, the basis of his dialectical logic. Its expansion and development, however, were largely conditioned by non-Platonic factors. The fact that such an interest is not found in Plato until these later works is perhaps indication enough for us that it was not of as central importance for Plato as Hegel wished to believe. Dialectic was not for the author of the dialogues nor is it for us today "the only truth and the only interest" in Plato's philosophy. At this point one cannot avoid the conviction that Hegel's extreme passion for logic prejudiced his historical judgment.

Plato had correctly apprehended the essential nature and truth of the intellectual world, but in addition to an inadequate mode of presentation, Hegel thought that his treatment fell short because he remained too exclusively concentrated upon universal determinations, and had only imperfectly applied the idea to the individual and the particular. In more formal Hegelian language, Plato remained in the objective, the sphere of the substantial only. It was Aristotle who first added the notion of subjectivity and concrete particularity in the principle of process. What with Plato was abstractly intellectual, Aristotle made concretely rational. The principle of life by which the universals as potentialities became particular actualities was not fully realized in Plato. In distinction to Pythagorean numbers and Platonic Ideas, Aristotle made process valid.

When Hegel enters Aristotle's realm, he is more truly at home than in the dialogues of Plato. Though, as he himself complained, he had studied Aristotle in the most difficult and unsatisfactory modern edition, the Baseler Folioausgabe which was not accompanied by a Latin translation, it is safe to say that he penetrated more intimately into his thought than into that of any other philosopher. There is certainly no other thinker whom he regarded with such unqualified admiration and respect. It is impossible to miss his personal feeling of allegiance; it appears again and again in the *History of Philosophy* and throughout his other works. Aristotle is called "the teacher of the human race", to whom most of the philosophic and natural sciences are beholden for their beginnings and their characterization. "If we would be serious with philosophy, nothing would be more desirable than to lecture upon Aristotle, for he is of all the ancients the most deserving of study."[20] Hegel often said that his religious contemporaries' desire to return to Plato belonged to "the weaknesses of our time", but of Aristotle's metaphysics and psychology he said, "They have never been surpassed."

The best way to realize Hegel's remarkable intellectual affinity with Aristotle is to read his lectures on the major Aristotelian works. With Aristotle, Hegel shared the passion for knowledge for its own sake to a degree that has characterized few others in all history. Both combined avidity for facts with the most profound philosophic love for the theoretical. We cannot here dwell on the points of agreement between the two,[21] but it is perhaps worthwhile to quote a suggestive aphorism from Hegel's *Tagebuch* which shows his real Aristotelian spirit.

Sei keine Schlafmütze, sondern immer wach! (says Hegel in the broad Swabian idiom characteristic of his speech.) Denn wenn du eine Schlafmütze bist, so bist du blind und stumm. Bist du aber wach, so siehst du Alles, und sagst zu Allem, was es ist. Dieses aber ist die Vernunft und das Beherrschen der Welt.

[Be no sleepy-head, but keep awake! For being a sleepy-head, you will be blind and mute. But if you are awake, you perceive everything, and recognize everything for what it is. This is reason and the mastery of the world.][22]

Hegel found in Aristotle the quality which Rudolf Haym considered preeminently characteristic of Hegel himself, namely, the combination of the strongest empiricism and sense for the real with the highest degree of speculative power (Geistigkeit). Aristotle impressed Hegel as an enquirer who had the patience to examine all particular phenomena and the insight to construe them in such a way as to discover the most profound philosophic implications. He never ceased to wonder at the all-inclusiveness of Aristotle's interests, the range of his intellect, the thoroughness with which he handled all sides of knowledge. Yet along with encyclopedic inclusiveness, Aristotle always remained the philosopher.

> He sought to determine every object; but he penetrated ever further speculatively into the nature of the object. This object remained however in its concrete determination; seldom did he lead it back to abstract thought-determinations. Hence the study of Aristotle is inexhaustible.[23]

The contemporary prejudice against Aristotle which Hegel was most anxious to refute was the impression that Aristotle held to the empirical theory of knowledge, the idea of mind as passive, as a *tabula rasa* upon which impressions were written from without. Had not Aristotle said in *De Anima* that the understanding in reality is nothing before it thinks? And that reason is like a book on the pages of which nothing is at the outset actually written? It was analogies of this sort that gave rise to the whole modern epistemology of sensational empiricism. Hegel was certain that Aristotle had been completely misunderstood: that his similes had been pressed too far and made to mean the exact opposite of what he had intended. As in the case of Plato, modern historians seized upon the external image and illustration which they interpreted with complete disregard for the context and the purpose which as figurative expressions they were intended to serve. For Aristotle, mind was not a passive tablet but itself possessed power of initiative. And Aristotle's misinterpreted similes simply meant that mind is all things implicitly, yet it is nothing before activity occurs. Thus for Aristotle mind was a natural organism containing potentialities of reasoning activity. Its realization was conceived as function, activity rather than form, developing structure rather than disengaged intelligibility. It was in this, according to Hegel's judgment, that Aristotle's thought was a fulfilment of Plato. It was this which made his psychology unsurpassed even in the modern world.

In my opinion, the important thing about Hegel's interpretation of this Aristotelian psychology is that he fully grasped its organic basis, and did not permit the involved epistemological quarrels of his day to mislead him into seeing a dualism that did not exist in this functional conception. For Aristotle mind was not, as it so often was in the philosophy of Hegel's day, an inexplicable phenomenon outside of and separate from nature, but it was the highest development within nature, the crown of its purposiveness. *Nous* was nature's complete realization and entelechy.

In close relation to this interpretation and still more suggestive of Hegel's esteem for Aristotle was his estimate of the *Physics*. Here his polemic was directed not against false modern interpretations as in the case of *De Anima*, but against the fact that eighteenth century physical theory had completely disregarded Aristotle. The physicists of the generation before Hegel thought of Aristotle as belonging to an age before the dawn of science. But Hegel, like other post-Kantians, was sharply critical of modern physics. His analysis of Aristotelian natural philosophy shows how completely he rejected much of the accepted scientific theory of his time and how stubbornly he held to the conviction that in the larger issues Aristotle had been right and the Newtonians wrong.

The basic issue for Hegel, as we have indicated, was the Aristotelian conception of nature as a life, a totality of organic processes determined by immanent teleology. The moderns saw an atomistic universe controlled by external mechanical relations, but Aristotle envisioned the world as living, interacting processes. For Hegel the problems that mechanical physics left unanswered had been largely resolved by the simple determinations which were central for Aristotle: the concept of necessity and the concept of end, efficient and final causation. Aristotle had interpreted nature not as a collocation of independent atoms brought into relation by forces acting from without, but as a self-productive life whose end was within itself. He had comprehended the profound notion of life as an organism which independently propels itself, changes, develops, yet remains identical with itself. Its own inner unity and power exist because there is within it the idea of self-realization, of movement from potentiality to fulfilment. And this principle of self-realization or process was not discoverable by regarding the constituent parts of the organism, by breaking it down into chemical properties. In the *Physics* of Aristotle Hegel found what was to be a fundamental tenet of his own philosophy: that the truth is the whole.[24] Life in nature is a consequence of the whole structure, and the elements are to be explained by reference to that whole and not the other way around.

The whole in terms of function is present in every member, as every member is in its way the whole, each in a different way. It is impossible to conceive a single categorial essence without conceiving at the same time the whole. Its structure is not enclosed in its own independent being, but in that of the entire system.[25]

That, in Hartmann's words, is the dominant insistence of Hegel, and it does not require special insight to recognize its origin in Aristotle's natural philosophy.

But this is not all that Hegel found in Aristotle. The conception of the active intellect in *De Anima* and, even more, the doctrine of the unmoved Mover in Book Λ of the *Metaphysics* formed for Hegel the highest point in Aristotle's understanding of the intellectual world. His deep desire to find a harmony between the individual and the objective world, his intellectual passion to comprehend all things, not as foreign to the human spirit, but as its material and its very substance, perceived in these Aristotelian speculations a final wisdom. It was not that Hegel interpreted these disputed passages in terms of transcendence; for him they embodied the most inclusive context within which this process of union of subject and object could be operative.

Man united with his world, his sense of being at home there, could come about, in the last analysis, only by thought and the power of reason. There the thinking self could entirely appropriate its object, the object of thought could be one with the thinker. The very nature of thought raised to its highest level in philosophy was reflection on self or self-consciousness. That became in Hegel's vision the goal of intellectual history. In the Aristotelian idea of mind, separate, unmixed, self-contained, whose essence was pure activity and whose activity was self-reflection, Hegel found the highest idealism that had ever yet been advocated. At the very end of his *Enzyklopädie*, the summing up of his whole system, Hegel quoted the famous passage from chapter seven of Book Λ. It is his acknowledgment of the fact that nothing better could be said, that this is the conclusion of the whole matter.

And thinking in itself deals with that which is best in itself, and that which is thinking in the fullest sense with that which is best in the fullest sense. And thought thinks on itself because it shares the nature of the object of thought; for it becomes an object of thought in coming into contact with and thinking its objects, so that thought and object of thought are the same. For that which is *capable* of receiving the object of thought, i.e. the essence, is thought. But it is *active* when it *possesses* this object. Therefore the possession rather than the receptivity is the divine element which thought seems to contain, and the act of contemplation is what is most pleasant and best.[26]

This is Hegel's answer to the dualisms of God and world, transcendence and immanence, thought and being. Here for him Plato and Aristotle came together, and here they anticipated the truth of the Christian faith. In these speculative reaches Plato and Aristotle attained to the true nature of the divine. Aristotle's searching spirit, at one with his teacher's, had comprehended "the empirical in its synthesis", and reached the highest speculative standpoint.

But if this can be said, in one sense, to be the ideal union of the spirit with its world, it is also for Hegel, as for Aristotle, an advance beyond it. For here the main emphasis on organic totality, the interrelatedness of all parts, is forsaken, and thought becomes complete in itself, a separate, self-enclosed activity. This signifies, on Hegel's part, passing beyond the social and natural world, dispensing with the material, eternalizing the process of reason. It is a union of the thought of Plato and Aristotle which if carried too far could destroy the sounder bases of the philosophy of both. Moreover, this conception of the self-completeness of reason is foreign to the main bent of the German thinker's whole evolutionary philosophy. It is an influence that has undeniably important consequences, upon which we have no occasion here to enter, though in any elaboration of Hegel's system of logic or of his analysis of the doctrines of Christianity, the importance of this Aristotelian-Platonic speculation would become obvious.

But Aristotle's philosophy was not built up logically around this single book of the *Metaphysics*. That fact constituted a problem for Hegel. Though he tried to insist that the works of Aristotle formed "a totality of purely speculative philosophy", he was too honest a critic to overlook the unsystematic and ununified character of this body of thought. "A system of philosophy is what we cannot find in Aristotle." Hegel appears to be always trying to conceive Aristotle as a whole, yet finding it impossible.

> And yet it cannot be denied (he concludes) that with Aristotle the object was not to bring everything to a unity or to reduce determinations to a unity of opposites, but, on the contrary, to retain each in its determination, and thus to pursue it further.[27]

Herein lies the great difference between the two thinkers. What separates Hegel from Aristotle most definitely is his desire for unity, for synthesis, for system as against Aristotle's equally strong desire for distinctions, for analytic investigation, for subject-matter in its discreteness. Aristotle's aporetic method could hardly be further in intention from Hegel's dialectical logic.

The *Organon*, Aristotle's logic, is the very antithesis to the philosophic method which Hegel approved. For here dialectic is not the instrument to discover truth, but rather its opposite, the prototype of the *Raisonniren* of the Enlightenment. It is precisely the method which Hegel was attempting to escape. In his history of philosophy Hegel treated the *Organon* in an unusual way. Giving up his three-fold division into Logic, Philosophy of Nature, and Philosophy of Spirit, he placed the *Metaphysics* first and brought the *Organon* in at the very end in a fourth division, as pendent to the rest.

Yet Hegel did not intend to deny the value of Aristotle's logic; he even maintained that this "natural history of finite thought" testified to the breadth of understanding of its originator. What he did deny was that Aristotle had thought in terms of the syllogisms of his own logic. The truths that Hegel found in the *Physics, De Anima,* and the *Metaphysics,* on the strength of which he believed Aristotle to be the highest speculative thinker, could not have been contained in the deductive logic of the *Analytics* or *Categories.* He concluded that the *Organon* was valuable as general method for the natural sciences, jurisprudence, mathematics, and the like, but unfitted as an instrument for arriving at any valuable philosophic truth.

What then had Aristotle left for the succeeding centuries to accomplish? The question is difficult enough to answer, because of an inevitable paradox in Hegel's thought, which we have already considered in other connections. The problem was how to conceive the sphere of *absoluter Geist,* the ideal activity of art, religion and philosophy in relation to the social world. How could true thought have a history, how could the absolute be relative? On the one hand, Hegel repeatedly affirmed that in the modern world one could not be either a Platonist or an Aristotelian, for history had advanced, and philosophy as well as all other activities was a product of the age and spirit of a people. Yet, on the other hand, he emphasized again and again that the Greek thinkers, particularly Aristotle, had not been surpassed. From the standpoint of philosophic discovery this twilight philosopher of Greece represented ultimate and lasting truth. Though such truth could in different epochs have an outer history and development it was itself always the same in core and substance. In a real sense this paradox remained an unresolved problem of Hegel's thought.

A partial answer is to be found in his emphasis on the reforming and remolding effect of the present on tradition. Though the content and substance of past truth might persist, every new society needed to fit it into new forms and find it revealed in new contexts. And in addition from the standpoint of organization a deficiency remained for Hegel in the Aristotelian philosophy. Aristotle's whole philosophy, wrote Hegel,

> really requires recasting, so that all his determinations should be brought into a necessary systematic whole—not a systematic whole which is correctly divided into its parts, and in which no part is forgotten, all being set forth in their proper order, but one in which there is *one* living organic whole, in which each part is held to be a part, and the whole alone as such is true.[28]

The important lack in both Platonic and Aristotelian philosophy lay in the fact that the parts were not fused into a unity; one idea was not implicit throughout. Aristotle had discovered the "absolute Idea" in the *Metaphysics*, but he had placed it side by side with the rest. The truth of Plato's *Parmenides* had not been applied in the remainder of the dialogues. Plato and Aristotle had discovered the "Idea", to use Hegelian phraseology, that is, they had come to the realization of the unity of self-consciousness and essence. They had recognized Thought as the being of the world, the unity of subject and object in reflection. But their philosophies had not been penetrated by that speculative idea. "This is what a succeeding time had to accomplish."

As far as the ancient world was concerned, the time which at least partially performed this recasting was the period of Neoplatonism. Here at the very threshold of the modern world and on the eve of a new world-religion the promise of Greek philosophy was in a measure fulfilled. For Hegel the Christian faith was based on some of the best truths of Plato and Aristotle. How this came about and the role of the Alexandrian school of philosophy in effecting such a union must be our final consideration.

Some students of Hegel have long been inclined to find an important key to his philosophy in his interpretation of Neoplatonism. Had not Plotinus, Porphyry, Proclus and other leaders of this school appreciated the unity of the Platonic and Aristotelian thought and had they not brought it into the closest relationship with Christianity, as Hegel himself was to do at a later time? Hegel's answer to this seems to be that they only pointed the way to an end which they themselves could not reach. For though they succeeded in accomplishing what Plato and Aristotle could not do, in forsaking the method of reasoning from particular and sensuous images, and conceiving the unity of self-consciousness and being purely as Thought, they never made the necessary logical synthesis of the objective and subjective. For Hegel, Neoplatonism represented an advance in the comprehension of certain important concepts, particularly regarding the nature of the Trinity, and the union of God and man, rather than a fulfilment of the past, such as Plato and Aristotle had effected.

Above all, he wished to see in the Neoplatonists the overcoming of the estrangement of spirit and nature that entered into the Greek world along with its political decline, and so strongly marked the Roman epoch. His characterization of the Hellenistic period, and in general of the era preceding the rise of the Christian philosophy, is one of the most suggestive aspects of Hegel's interpretation of history. In his earliest writings, it will be remembered, he had been convinced that just here had occurred one of the most significant changes in human thought—a transformation which had caused men to break loose from traditional moorings and seek an absolute religion, though it was a foreign one. Now after a lifetime of study he was no less convinced of the importance of this time in changing the character of the world.

Stoicism, Epicureanism, and Scepticism reflected a sharp break between man and nature. They were not a development from Plato and Aristotle but represented a direct antithesis. The old feeling of being at home in the world was gone. The Hellenistic philosophers forsook the social to save their own souls; they withdrew into the seeming security of self. The temporal world became unreal and untrue. Only by complete indifference toward everything external could "the wise man" hope to possess his soul in peace. But the final development of a powerful scepticism destroyed even this last citadel, and left man utterly without self-certainty. Scepticism, the "surrender of everything objective, the absolute poverty of all content which could be established and secure", was evidence of the decay of both philosophy and civilization.

Hegel believed that Christianity, understood in its philosophical substance, offered a reconciliation to this world of "spirit in self-estrangement" which overcame the dualism that had so long separated man and nature. The subjective attitude of Stoics and Sceptics no longer satisfied mankind. Men found that they could not live in a private, isolated, atomistic sphere. The new idea that arose with Christianity, and which had been intimated before in ancient philosophy, was the concept that God or absolute existence "is nothing alien to self-consciousness, that nothing really exists for it in which self-consciousness is not itself immediately present."[29] Neoplatonism, in its absorption with Platonic, Pythagorean and Aristotelian theories, reflected to some degree this return of the spirit to its home in the objective world and the breaking down of the abstractions of self-contained existence.

> The fundamental idea in Neoplatonism (wrote Hegel) is Thought which is its own object, and which is therefore identical with its object, with what is thought; so that we have the one and the other and the unity of both.[30]

The Neoplatonists returned to the conception of the truth of the objective by means of pure thought, which built up the external spiritual world from within. They conceived of God as the absolutely objective, as Being, fully manifested and revealed to the human intellect, yet wholly self-contained and independent. This absolute objectivity was in its very nature spirit, implying eternal self-identical existence, which had nevertheless differentiated itself and created the world. Yet man in so far as he was mind represented the return to this primal unity of God. For the Neoplatonists the absolute was outside themselves as eternal universal truth, but it was not unrelated to man. The world as the "other" of God was not himself, but as God's activity it was a phase or moment of himself.

Such, in brief, is the substance of Hegel's interpretation of Neoplatonism. He did not consider the writings of Plotinus and Proclus an advance upon Plato and Aristotle, but a special development from the logical and metaphysical truths expressed in *Parmenides* and Book Λ of the *Metaphysics*. Hegel defended Plotinus from the charge of mysticism often brought against his conception of God as pure Being in which potentiality and actuality coincided. This pure intellectualism seemed to Hegel inconsistent with the idea of mysticism. While he approved of many aspects of the *Enneads* he objected to their arbitrariness of idea and inadequate imagery which sometimes seemed to take the place of conceptual thought. From this standpoint his successor, Proclus, appeared more significant to Hegel because of his closer attention to Plato's logic. He had uncovered in the *Parmenides* what Hegel called "the true theology, the real revelation of all mysteries of the divine essence." This true theology, the concept of the Trinity, had become the central truth of Christianity. This truth implicit in Plato's dialectic revealed the nature of the world as the unity of the one and the many, or the universal and the particular in the organic concept of becoming. Hegel elaborated in wearisome detail the determination of the triads of Proclus and the trinity of trinities. Into these disquisitions we have no need to follow. Suffice it to say that Proclus' essential principle was conceived to be God as spirit, spirit concrete and determined in kind by the idea of the dialectical nature of truth.

But in Hegel's opinion the Neoplatonists had not grasped the Christian truth of the value of the individual. They had not gone from man as a concrete type to man as a particular person. Though they recognized the true nature of spirit, and represented the absolute totality as concrete, Alexandrian philosophy had not gone further toward the recognition of the individual's intrinsic worth and freedom. For Hegel that remained the distinctive contribution of the Christian religion. Also the rationalism of the Neoplatonists prevented them from developing the natural side, the sphere of objective mind, the life of society. Their systems were in no sense adequate and complete because they had grasped only the speculative essence of the ancients.

Moreover, the unity which they had found—and this is Hegel's most insistent criticism—was not a unity really grounded in the true dialectic, the recognition of the absolute chasm separating thesis and antithesis. Theirs in the last analysis was an abstract identity of subject and object, not a maintenance of the separate phases in organic totality. Their philosophy lacked the inner necessity of dialectical determination. Therefore, it can be safely concluded that for Hegel the Neoplatonists did not actually succeed in recasting the Aristotelian and Platonic philosophies into a system fully in accord with the revelations contained in their speculative reaches. Such re-forming had to await a later time than that of the Neoplatonists. It was eventually undertaken by Hegel himself who attempted to carry through substantially this process in his *Science of Logic*.[31]

So Hegel summed up the history of Greek philosophy from Thales to Proclus. In spite of his dialectical scheme, it did not for him take the form of a necessary progress from thinker to thinker. Rather it became the record of an expanding and deepening knowledge, a wisdom in which each trend and each school made its contribution to the whole.

CONCLUSION

The pathos of history, the sorrow and sense of futility that descend upon the reflective man when he sees the past as "the slaughter-bench" at which the happiness, wisdom and virtue of individuals and states have been victimized,—such were the striking terms in which Hegel characterized the sharp decline that followed the brief glory of Hellas. But from this partial view his philosophic mind penetrated the more inclusive whole, in which tragedy and defeat are but a phase. From his need to understand the complexity of the human record, he evolved a system of metaphysics which attempted to account for the totality of experience. This metaphysics can be best appreciated as a comprehensive mythology derived from a sustained vision of history. Hegel himself, one of the wisest and most subtle minds of modern times, did not intend his dialectical system to be understood in any literal sense, a pitfall that has beset the path of many of his followers. For him it was a universal medium, a method of interpreting the meaning of events in time. Like Christian dogma it is true to man's deeper and recurring experiences rather than to literal fact or to isolated outward occurrences. In common with the sanest and most penetrating thinkers before him, Hegel recognized that man's art and philosophy and religion are but inadequate expressions of truths too far-reaching to be comprehended by any single mind. It is the fate of human thought to be partial and one-sided, to see forever in a glass darkly. This Hegel knew but he was also aware that collective human experience enables men to see more and more inclusive unities and wider inter-relationships, and so to move from the partial to the more complete.

Hegel's studies of Greek religion, ethics and philosophy show him to have been a relatively unbiased critic of past ideas in spite of his dialectical scheme and his absolutist metaphysics. On the whole his speculative theories did not pervert the truth of his subject matter. He used them as a kind of framework, the function of which was to set the larger context in perspective both for himself and his readers. If he had been fettered by the logic of his own system, he would have been compelled to see an advance in the modern world over the Greek. Actually, however, he could concede only a partial and limited progress. As a mature philosopher he was certain that Christianity had passed beyond the insights of Greek humanism in its evaluation of the individual. But it was his lasting conviction that modern Christian civilization had gone to an extreme in placing supreme value on the individual person and his subjective claims, to the serious detriment of culture as a whole and higher truth. He believed that in all history the Greeks alone had grasped the essential relation of subject and universal. What they had lacked was a thoroughly humanized religion, a religion supporting the sacredness and importance of individuality, and also giving assurance of a wholly intelligible deity. Such a religion must abolish forever the unintelligibility of blind fate and the sway of mere nature. Christianity, in Hegel's Hellenized interpretation of it, supplied this imperative need.

The idea most basic to Hegel's philosophy of history, an idea derived directly from classical culture, is the concept of freedom or self-realization attained through progress from the subjective and inward to the objective and substantial. The mind as subjectivity is merely nature that is not unfolded. It is abstract, implicit, isolated. As actual or real, the mind is concrete, explicit, objective. Freedom, in Hegel's view, is achieved to the degree that man becomes at home in his society, in his cultural inheritance, and in the spiritual universe as a whole. Both for the individual and for the race freedom is a movement from the isolated to the implicated. Religion and art and philosophy are forms of explicit expression that further this universal purpose. Particular religions, the various arts, and philosophies serve as measures of the degree of freedom which a national culture has attained. They are different embodiments of one general content which is the all-embracing intelligibility of the real world. The realization of freedom means that an individual has become aware of the spiritual whole and of his relation to it. For Hegel that whole and that relation found fullest incarnation in public institutions, which he considered to be both the gauge and consequence of a people's life.

He was convinced that the modern world could not escape its inner contradictions and overcome its error of individualism without reference to this Greek insight into the nature of freedom. Only by taking account of that recognition of the organic relations of man and his world could a higher advance be made toward this goal. Only by combining the new truth brought by Christianity with the older humanism revealed in Greek culture could a better synthesis be achieved. That Hegel himself sought to bring about this synthesis in his ethics and metaphysics has, I hope, become clear in the foregoing pages. In the end he wished to believe that nothing of worth in history is irrevocably lost. Truths which the past revealed were renewed in wider horizons of consciousness. Though the external bloom of Greece was long gone, the fruits her people had ripened were preserved and purveyed to the present by the venerable housekeeper, Tradition. Viewed from the vantage point of national life, the essential values were woven into the institutions and practices of modern society.

From the vantage point of the individual thinker, all of the past was the property of the present, and the present was as rich and full as the seeker, earnest and unafraid, could make it. Hegel's was a faith, secure and impregnable, that did not shrink from pain and tragedy, a belief that out of pain and tragedy could arise the most sublime of human values. History became for him, much as it was for Herder, a "holy chain" in which the past was united with the present. History was not moving away from a paradise nor yet moving toward one, and mankind was always and yet never at its end and goal.

But to envision the unity of the past within the present and to set it forth in a great philosophical synthesis did not accomplish this unity in fact. To this the subsequent history of Hegel's ideas bears eloquent testimony. Though he believed he had brought into harmonious relationship the positive insights of classical and Christian ages, the years since Hegel's time have hardly borne out his faith. The problem of evaluating the individual in the light of the social whole; the problem of conceiving religion as a unification and transmutation of human ideals; the problem of understanding the natural and the intellectual world as an interlocking totality and process —these are still vexed and troubled issues today. Because of the effect of the industrial and technological revolutions in breaking the continuity of tradition, these problems have grown more, rather than less, perplexing. We have not yet learned to be at home in our world—Hegel's fondest dream; we have not yet fused the contradictory elements of our Greek and Christian inheritance. But Hegel's thought has profoundly influenced modern life and has aided in bringing about the recognition of Greek naturalistic ideals. Whether those ideals can be incorporated more closely into our individualistic ethic and our religious tradition has still to be decided. Hegel's unquestioned value seems to lie, most clearly, in his having brought these problems to light.

NOTES

1. *Philosophie der Geschichte* (Glockner Jubiläumsausgabe, 1927).
   S. 48, 49; Sibree translation pp. 21, 22.
   I have followed substantially the accepted English translations of Hegel's works, except for the *Jugendschriften* where none are yet available. However, I have taken the liberty to make occasional changes, especially in the lowering of upper-case letters. Many of the older translators seemed to read Hegel in terms of capital nouns only. These changes can be noted by referring to the works themselves which are in every instance cited both in English and German. The Glockner edition has been used, except where otherwise indicated. Naturally, its text does not in every case agree with that of the edition from which the translations were made, but the differences in the selections quoted are not great.

2. *Ibid.,* S. 34; p. 9.

3. Cf. Lessing's, *Die Erziehung des Menschengeschlechts,* Kant's *Idee zu einer allgemeinen Geschichte in weltbürgerlicher Absicht,* and Herder's *Ideen zur Philosophie der Geschichte der Menschheit.*

4. *Philosophie der Geschichte,* S. 37; p. 11.

5. *Ibid.,* S. 50, 51; p. 22.

6. *Ibid.,* S. 52; p. 23.

7. *Geschichte der Philosophie,* Bd. I, S. 22; E. S. Haldane translation, Vol. I, p. XIII.

8. *Philosophie der Geschichte,* S. 71; p. 39.

9. *Ästhetik,* Bd. I, S. 142; Osmaston trans., Vol. I, p. 133.

10. *Philosophie der Geschichte,* S. 90, 91; p. 55.

11. *Ibid.,* S. 113, 114; p. 74.

12. I have used the order of hierarchy found in the *Ästhetik,* I, S. 139 ff., since it seemed more relevant to the concept of "Volksgeist" than the somewhat different arrangement in the *Philosophie des Rechts.*

13. Cf. Kurt Leese, *Die Geschichtsphilosophie Hegels,* S. 110.

14. *Philosophie der Geschichte,* S. 79; p. 46.

15. Georg Lasson's revised edition of the *Philosophie der Geschichte* in the "Philosophische Bibliothek," S. 105; my trans.

16. *Philosophie der Geschichte,* S. 84, 85; p. 50.

17. *Ibid.,* S. 116; p. 76.

18. This contrast between an organic conception and a dialectical one,

which seems to me fairly obvious in Hegel's thinking, is denied by many Hegelian scholars. They point out that for Hegel organic life is itself dialectical; cf. the Introduction to the *Phenomenology of Spirit* and the famous correspondence between Hegel and Goethe on this matter. Hegel did attempt to apply dialectic to all phenomena, natural and spiritual. But it seems to me apparent, though not explicit, that in his philosophy of history the dialectical and the organic conceptions are set over against each other, the former as peculiar to the life of spirit, the latter as characteristic of the life of nature and of cultures when they are considered separately, i.e., not in historical progression and interrelation. This problem is central to the Hegelian point of view, but the limits of this study permit only the indication, not the development, of it.

19. *Philosophie der Geschichte*, S. 119; p. 78.
20. Germanic understood as medieval and modern European.
21. Cf. Wilhelm Dilthey, *Die Jugendgeschichte Hegels*. My indebtedness to Dilthey's general point of view regarding Hegel here and in the following chapter will be apparent to the student of Dilthey's thought. I consider his interpretation of German philosophy, in its grasp of essentials, as belonging to the best critical work yet written in the field.
22. *Philosophie der Geschichte*, S. 119, 120; pp. 78, 79.

CHAPTER II: YOUNG HEGEL'S DISCOVERY OF THE GREEKS

1. Rosenkranz, *Hegels Leben, Supplement*, S. 458.
2. The differentiation between Greek and Roman cultures was later to become a major consideration in Hegel's philosophy of history. Winckelmann first tried to draw a clear distinction but in the Germany of Hegel's youth such discrimination seems not to have been general.
3. Rosenkranz, *op. cit.*, S. 460.
4. Quoted in Theodor Haering's *Hegel, sein Wollen und sein Werk*, S. iii.
5. *Hegel und der Staat*, 1920.
6. The genetic studies that have thus far been made fail to reveal any agreement regarding the chronology of the manuscripts. Nohl's collation disagrees with Dilthey's critical analysis, and Haering's study disagrees with both. It is difficult, perhaps impossible, to determine which fragments belong to the Bern and which to the Frankfurt years. Though I may be presumptuous in not accepting Haering's dating, I have not attempted to consider the passages chronologically, but have arranged them in the order best suited for my purpose.
7. Nohl, S. 26. Translations in this chapter are mine.

8. Nohl, S. 28.
9. Nohl, S. 215.
10. Nohl, S. 27.
11. Nohl, S. 2.
12. Nohl, S. 23.
13. Nohl, S. 246.
14. Nohl, S. 255.
15. Nohl, S. 260.
16. Fragments included under the title "Der Geist des Christentums und sein Schicksal." They are assigned by Dilthey and Haering to Hegel's later *Hauslehrer* period; hence they were probably written in the last years of the 18th century.
17. Nohl, S. 221.
18. Nohl, S. 223.
19. Nohl, S. 223.
20. Nohl, S. 225.
21. Quoted in Theodor Haering, *op. cit.*, S. iii.

CHAPTER III: THE RELIGION OF BEAUTY

1. Cf. Michael Foster, *Die Geschichte als Schicksal des Geistes in der Hegelschen Philosophie*, or Franz Rosenzweig, *op. cit.* for a detailed consideration of this change.
2. *Geschichte der Philosophie*, Bd. I, S. 187, 188; Haldane trans. Vol. I, p. 150.
3. Cf. W. Rehm, *Griechentum und Goethezeit* for a recent, interesting treatment of neo-Hellenism, with emphasis on the gradual overcoming of the first estimates of Greece.
4. Osmaston's trans., found in Vol. II, p. 269, of *The Philosophy of Fine Art*.
5. *Philosophie der Geschichte*, S. 315; p. 239.
6. *Ibid.*, S. 310; p. 235.
7. *Ibid.*, S. 314; p. 239.
8. *Ästhetik*, Bd. II, S. 55; Vol. II, p. 219.
9. *Ibid.*, Bd. II, S. 55; Vol. II, p. 219.
10. *Philosophie der Religion*, Bd. I, S. 160; Speirs trans., Vol. II, p. 293.
11. *Ibid.*, Bd. II, S. 127; Vol. II, pp. 257, 258.
12. *Ästhetik*, Bd. I, S. 151; p. 142.

CHAPTER IV: THE HELLENIC SOCIAL ETHOS

1. *Ästhetik*, Bd. II, S. 52; Osmaston trans., Vol. II, p. 215.
2. *Geschichte der Philosophie*, Bd. I, S. 189; Vol. I, p. 151.

3. *Philosophie der Geschichte*, S. 330; p. 253.

4. *Geschichte der Philosophie*, Bd. II, S. 33; Vol. I, p. 409.

5. This forms, as we have seen, the basic theme of the Hegelian interpretation of tragedy. Friedrich Hebbel made use of this theory, and his two dramas, *Herodes und Mariamne* and *Gyges und sein Ring*, remind us of this conception of Socrates as a man who had advanced beyond the understanding of the age in which he lived and fell victim, not unjustly, to the substantial powers of that age.

6. *Geschichte der Philosophie*, Bd. II, S. 116; Vol. I, p. 441.

7. Cf. M. B. Foster, *The Political Philosophies of Plato and Hegel* for a valuable, if not always acceptable, treatment of the subject.

8. *Geschichte der Philosophie*, Bd. II, S. 272; Vol. II, p. 93.

9. *Philosophie des Rechts*, S. 266; Dyde trans., pp. 188, 189.

10. *Ibid.*, S. 324; p. 252.

11. It is significant that Hegel's interpretation of Platonic ethics is based almost wholly on the *Republic*, rather than on the later dialogues. Though there is a reference or two in his writings to the *Laws*, he seems not to have taken account of their radical differences from the point of view of the *Republic*, particularly in the matter of private, subjective freedom. For Hegel, Plato represented the "substantial Idea" in ethics and was lacking entirely the concept of subjectivity as a valid part of freedom.

12. Foster, *op.cit.*, p. 116.

13. Cf. George Sabine, *A History of Political Theory*, Chap. XXX. A recent, excellent chapter on Hegel to which I am indebted.

CHAPTER V: MINERVA'S OWL

1. *Geschichte der Philosophie*, Bd. I, S. 51, 52; Vol. I, p. 23.

2. *Ibid.*, S. 29; p. 2, 3.

3. Cf. Sabine, *op. cit.*, p. 632 ff.

4. *Philosophie des Rechts*, S. 36, 37; p. xxx.

5. *Geschichte der Philosophie*, Bd. II, S. 182; Vol. II, pp. 13, 14.

6. Nicolai Hartmann, in his study *Aristoteles und Hegel*, 1933, brings out the fact that Hegel was attempting to combine, in this doctrine of the concrete, the speculations of Plato and Aristotle. With Plato he maintained that truth of being is only the essence, the universal; with Aristotle he emphasized the developing, immanent nature of all universals in concrete content. Hartmann points out, quite rightly, that in his conception of the inadequacy of the logical to exhaust the total nature of anything, Aristotle allows a place for individuality which Hegel on his premises cannot admit. For Aristotle the definition does

not reveal the whole nature of the real, whereas for Hegel the logical idea includes not only the common genus, but all the differentiating marks of the species as well. Hence the idea contains all that is real in any given content, and individual uniqueness becomes merely phenomenal. This attempted union of the thought of Plato and Aristotle accounts, in my opinion, for a great deal of the doubleness of Hegel's emphases.

7. It should be noted that this is not the dialectical, triadic organization of the history of Greek philosophy which Hegel undertook, but which he pursued half-heartedly, and which seems fairly irrelevant.

8. *Wissenschaft der Logik*, Bd. I, S. 118; Johnston and Struthers trans., Vol. I, p. 117.

9. In this connection he drew the important distinctions between the conclusions of Zeno and Kant, also between the scepticism of the later academies and eighteenth-century scepticism. The Greeks never doubted that reason applied to existence and that its knowledge of the world was real. They knew no epistemological dualism between thought and being.

10. *Geschichte der Philosophie*, Bd. I, S. 350; Vol. I, p. 283.

11. In the case of Aristotle, Hegel was at some pains to trace the various traditions through Cicero, Alexandrian philosophy, the medieval period, and the modern, but in the case of Plato his polemic against tradition was generally not specific. The modern false opinions regarding both thinkers were well represented for Hegel by Tennemann's *Geschichte der Philosophie*, and also by Dietrich Tiedmann's and J. J. Brucker's Histories. Hegel was also in direct opposition to the work of Schleiermacher and to the Romantic religious interest in Plato. In this connection and in the light of Hegel's critique, it is hard to understand what Professor Stace, in his recent book, *The Philosophy of Hegel*, means by calling Hegel's interpretation of Plato "traditional".

12. *Geschichte der Philosophie*, Bd. II, S. 170; Vol. II, p. 9.

13. *Ibid.*, S. 170; p. 9.

14. *Ibid.*, S. 189; p. 20.

15. *Ibid.*, S. 179; p. 10.

16. Hegel did not specifically defend his monistic interpretation of Plato nor specifically attack the dualistic tradition, but it is clear from his constant criticism of a too literal reading of the dialogues, especially of the myths, where the dualistic conceptions have largely been supported. Moreover, he not infrequently referred to the Platonic idea of the "soul and body as cast in one nature, and the divine and eternal as just this purity in which soul and body are of one piece". H.

Glockner asserts, however, quite inexplicably to me, that Hegel interpreted Plato as a "dualist". Cf. *Hegel,* Bd. I, S. 108.

17. *Geschichte der Philosophie,* Bd. II, S. 226, 227; Vol. II, p. 53.

18. *Ibid.,* S. 237; p. 67.

19. *Wie Hegel Plato auffaszt,* in the "Philosophische Monatshefte" VII, 1871, 72.

20. *Geschichte der Philosophie,* Bd. II, S. 314; Vol. II, p. 134.

21.   Nicolai Hartmann has done that rather well in the book already mentioned, *Aristoteles und Hegel,* in which he maintains that Leibniz and Hegel are the only Aristotelians—in the sense of original thinkers —of modern times.

22. Rosenkranz, *op. cit.,* S. 540.

23. *Geschichte der Philosophie,* Bd. II, S. 314; Vol. II, p. 134.

24.   A passage from the *Phenomenology of Spirit* is relevant here. Hegel emphasized the importance of purpose or end in Aristotle's natural philosophy together with the process by which it is attained.

> For the real subject-matter is not exhausted in its purpose, but in working the matter out; nor is the mere result attained the concrete whole itself, but the result along with the process of arriving at it. The purpose by itself is a lifeless universal, just as the general drift is a mere activity in a certain direction, which is still without its concrete realization; and the naked result is the corpse of the system which has left its guiding tendency behind it.
>
>   *Phänomenologie des Geistes,* S. 13; Baillie trans. (second edition), p. 69.

25. N. Hartmann, *op. cit.,* S. 14.

26. Oxford trans. of the works of Aristotle, VIII, p. 1072b. A part only of the passage from Aristotle quoted by Hegel is here cited.

27. *Geschichte der Philosophie,* Bd. II, S. 314; Vol. II, p. 133.

28. *Ibid.,* S. 415, p. 223.

29. *Ibid.,* Bd. III, S. 4; Vol. II, p. 375.

30. *Ibid.,* S. 13, pp. 382, 383.

31. Cf. N. Hartmann, *op. cit.,* S. 38 et passim.

SELECTED BIBLIOGRAPHY

PRIMARY WORKS

Hegel, G. W. F.
  Sämtliche Werke. Jubiläumsausgabe in zwanzig Bänden, Ed. by Hermann Glockner, Stuttgart, 1927.
  Sämtliche Werke. Philosophische Bibliothek, Ed. by Georg Lasson, Leipzig, 1920.
  Hegel's theologische Jugendschriften, Ed. by Hermann Nohl, Tübingen, 1907.
  Hegel-Lexikon in vier Bänden, Ed. by Hermann Glockner, 1927 (incomplete).

TRANSLATIONS

Hegel's Philosophy of Mind, from the Encyclopaedia of the Philosophical Sciences. By W. Wallace, Oxford, 1894.
Lectures on the History of Philosophy. By E. S. Haldane and F. H. Simson, London, 1894. 3 Vols.
Lectures on the Philosophy of Religion. By E. B. Speirs and J. B. Sanderson, London, 1895, 3 Vols.
The Logic of Hegel. From the Encyclopaedia of the Philosophical Sciences. By W. Wallace, Oxford, 1892.
The Phenomenology of Mind. By J. B. Baillie, London, 1931.
The Philosophy of Fine Art. By F. P. B. Osmaston, London, 1920, 4 Vols.
The Philosophy of History. By J. Sibree, New York, 1900.
The Philosophy of Right. By S. W. Dyde, London, 1896.
The Science of Logic. By W. J. Johnston and L. G. Struthers, New York, 1929, 2 Vols.

CRITICAL WORKS

Adams, George P. The Mystical Element in Hegel's Early Theological Writings, Berkeley, 1910.
Bratuscheck, E. "Wie Hegel Plato auffasst", in Philosophische Monatshefte, Vol. VII, 1871, 72.
Dilthey, Wilhelm. Die Jugendgeschichte Hegels, Leipzig and Berlin, 1921.
Falkenheim, Hugo. Goethe und Hegel, Tübingen, 1934.
Fischer, Kuno. Hegels Leben, Werke und Lehre, Heidelberg, 1901.

Foster, Michael B. The Political Philosophies of Plato and Hegel, Oxford, 1935.

————. Die Geschichte als Schicksal des Geistes in der Hegelschen Philosophie, Tübingen, 1929.

Glockner, Hermann. Hegel. Die Voraussetzungen der Hegelschen Philosophie, Bd. I, Stuttgart, 1929.

Haering, Theodor. Hegel: sein Wollen und sein Werk, Leipzig, 1920. 2 Vols.

Hartmann, Nicolai. Die Philosophie des deutschen Idealismus. Hegel, Bd. II, Berlin, 1932.

————. Aristoteles und Hegel, Erfurt, 1933.

Haym, Rudolf. Hegel und seine Zeit, Berlin, 1857.

Hoffmeister, Johannes. Hölderlin und Hegel, Tübingen, 1931.

Lasson, Georg. Hegel als Geschichtsphilosoph, Leipzig, 1920.

Leese, Kurt. Die Geschichtsphilosophie Hegels, Berlin, 1922.

Loewenberg, Jacob. Introduction to Hegel: Selections, New York, 1929.

Maier, Josef. On Hegel's Critique of Kant, New York, 1939.

Rehm, Wilhelm. Griechentum und Goethezeit, Leipzig, 1936.

Reyburn, Hugh A. The Ethical Theory of Hegel, Oxford, 1921.

Rosenkranz, Karl. Hegels Leben, Berlin, 1826.

Rosenzweig, Franz. Hegel und der Staat, München, 1920. 2 Vols.

Royce, Josiah. Lectures on Modern Idealism, New Haven, 1919.

Sabine, George H. A History of Political Theory, New York, 1937.

Stace, W. T. The Philosophy of Hegel, London, 1924.

Stefansky, Georg. Das hellenisch-deutsche Weltbild. Einleitung in die Lebensgeschichte Schellings, Bonn, 1925.

Stenzel, Johannes. "Hegels Auffassung der griechischen Philosophie" in Verhandlungen des Hegelkongresses. II, Berlin, 1932.

INDEX

UNIVERSITY OF CALIFORNIA PUBLICATIONS

IN

PHILOSOPHY

Vol. 2, No. 4, pp. 67-102   September 24, 1910

THE MYSTICAL ELEMENT IN HEGEL'S EARLY THEOLOGICAL WRITINGS

BY

GEORGE PLIMPTON ADAMS.

The study of the writings of Hegel before the Jena period has hitherto been possible only in a fragmentary way. Those writings which Rosenkranz has given in his biography of Hegel are too brief to give any adequate conception of the development of Hegel's own thinking in the decade from 1790 to 1800. Moreover, that the final system as given in the *Logic* really had a history, a genesis, really ever appeared in a more humane and less scholastic form, has always been difficult to appreciate, so massively overwhelming has the system seemed both to friend and foe.

The recent publication of all of Hegel's extant early theological writings, critically edited by Dr. Herman Nohl,[1] may well renew our interest in whatever beginnings and tentative forms the later system may have had. These writings have a significance for the student of Hegel which should not be underestimated. They make possible a first-hand acquaintance with the gradual development of the Hegelian system in the mind of its author. They let us see the motives which influenced the philosopher in their original ruggedness and purity, devoid of

---

[1] *Hegel's theologische Jugendschriften*, herausgegeben von Dr. Herman Nohl, Tübingen, 1907. I am indebted to the monograph of Dilthey, "Die Jugendgeschichte Hegels," in *Abhandlungen der Königlich Preussischen Akademie der Wissenschaften*, 1905, based upon an independent study of all the manuscripts which Nohl has published. This throws light upon much in these early writings that would otherwise have been obscure.

the scholastic and technical trappings of the later writings. They permit a just appreciation of the experiential core of the system. Indeed, one might come away from a study of these early writings feeling that the *Logic* of the mature Hegel is nothing but a highly elaborated and formal account of what the younger Hegel felt and lived in a concrete and vivid way. The insight expressed in these early writings is the real stuff, the real contents of the later system, however self-contained and self-adequate the latter may appear to be. Whatever fate awaited the later Hegel, the younger Hegel conceived of his philosophy as a sympathetic criticism of life, and not as the logical construction of a rational system.

There are, one may say, two different motives in the pursuit of philosophy; they represent two different types of mind in thinkers who deserve to be called philosophers. The one type chooses to explore the life, the spirit, the *Geist,* of some definite region of human activity expressing some universal human interest: I mean that any attempt sympathetically to summarize the inner life and soul of any fundamental human interest, such as religion, literature, art, science, or politics, in any one epoch or man or movement,—that such an attempt is truly a philosophical task. The other type, more exploited in the histories of philosophy, seeks to dwell in the atmosphere of thought, constructing its own system by logical necessity and rigid metaphysics. The contrast between these two types is the contrast between the historical and the systematic, the experiential and the *a priori* method.

The Hegelian philosophy is usually considered to be the quintessence of the metaphysical, logical, and *a priori* method. Pfleiderer, for instance, says: ''The exclusively logical character of Hegel's philosophy, with its resolution of all life into conceptual relations and processes of thought, is the ground of the weakness of his theory of religion, *viz.,* its bare intellectual character, its exclusive accentuation of the religious *concept,* and its failure to see that religion is essentially a matter of the heart.''[2]   It is with reference to just this judgment that these early writings of Hegel are significant. They enable us to see that

―――――――――
[2] Pfleiderer, *The Development of Modern Theology,* page 73.

in its early form, at one well-defined period of his development, Hegel's philosophy was through and through of the first type.[3] It was historical and not logical, experiential and not metaphysical. The critical work of Dr. Nohl in arranging the manuscripts chronologically lets us see the limits of this period in a much clearer way than could be gathered from the accounts of either Rosenkranz or Haym. They let us see something of the motives which led Hegel into sympathy for mysticism and even romantic enthusiasm during this period. Hegel, as we know, in his *Phenomenology,* repudiated all such mysticism and romantic *Schwärmerei;* and his *Logic* seems to be as remote as possible from any primitive mysticism and immediate intuition. However, in the light of subsequent developments, perhaps the most interesting and significant problem in the interpretation of the Hegelian philosophy, and indeed of all absolute idealisms, is precisely this relation between the two motives of intuition and discursive thought, experience and its intellectual elaboration, mysticism and rationalism. Hegel's philosophy is in reality a double system of bookkeeping, one entry being the symbolizing and expression, half artistic and half artificial, of some of the deepest and most universal aspects of concrete human experience; the other entry being a metaphysical and logical construction, partly out of these and partly out of other elements.[4]

---

[3] Cf. Haym, *Hegel und seine Zeit,* p. 48: "Hier, wenn irgendwo, in dieser einzigen Methode, sich über einen bedeutsamen Stoff zu verständigen, kann man die Natur des Hegel'schen Geistes und die Genesis seiner Überzeugungen belauschen. Sein Denken ist nicht ein von Begriffen zu Begriffen fortgehendes, sondern aus Anschauung und Empfindung zu Begriffen sich zuspitzendes."

[4] Eucken speaks of the conflict in Hegel between a more immediate living intuition (*lebendige Anschauung geistiger Wirklichkeit*) and the system which is through and through intellectualistic and logical (*eine Verwandelung der ganzen Wirklichkeit in ein Gewebe logischer Beziehungen*). Cf. *Die Lebensanschauungen der grossen Denker,* p. 458. Eucken does not, however, see any intimate relation between these two opposing factors, but regards them more or less as foreign to each other. James has called attention to the part which immediate intuition plays in Hegel's philosophy. Cf. *A Pluralistic Universe,* p. 93: "But what he really worked by was his own empirical perceptions, which exceeded and overflowed his miserably insufficient logical categories in every instance of their use." James, however, emphasizes the immediate intuition of the negativity and relativity, the sublation of things, rather than the more definitely religious mysticism which is revealed in these hitherto uncollected writings. Cf. also Dilthey, *Jugendgeschichte,* p. 153, who has some excellent words upon this problem of the relation between the logical and the mystical in Hegel.

A review of these early writings shows pretty clearly that there was a period in Hegel's development when he felt that a thorough-going mysticism is alone adequate to deal with either morality or religion. This mystical period was preceded by a period of rather complete acceptance of the Kantian and the Enlightenment ideas of morality and religion. But throughout this earlier and non-mystical period there emerges an increasing sympathy with certain motives of mysticism, an increasing distrust of the adequacy of the Kantian and Enlightenment philosophy of religion. It is a study of these non-Kantian, or mystical, elements and their culmination in the period of full-fledged mysticism, which is here undertaken.

That Hegel during his later years at Tübingen, and during his tutorship in Bern, came under the influence of rationalism and of the Enlightenment, of Lessing and of Kant, so that he interpreted religion in the Kantian manner and wrote, for instance, a life of Jesus much in the spirit of Kant,—all of this Rosenkranz and Haym have made clear. A series of somewhat scattered fragments, covering some seventy printed pages and frequently obscure, are grouped together by Nohl under the title of *Volksreligion und Christentum.* These belong, at least many of them, to Hegel's last year at Tübingen. The interest and significance of these earliest theological writings lie in their witness to the way in which the youthful theologian reacted to the overpowering influence of the great Kantian conceptions of reason, autonomy, and freedom; or, rather, to those embodiments of the eighteenth century Enlightenment which became crystallized in Kant. While the dominant motive running through these writings is the Kantian conception of *Vernunftreligion* and moral autonomy, expressions of a very different motive are constantly appearing. These indicate the motive which culminates in Hegel's mystical pantheism of the end of the decade, and show that at one time he had a great deal of sympathy for the romantic spirit; they let us see that Hegel had passed through just that romantic mysticism against which he contends in the preface of the *Phenomenology.* There are, then, in these earliest fragments, these two strands, which we shall call the Kantian, and the non-Kantian,[5] the rationalistic and the mystical.

There are two chief non-Kantian motives in these early writings: first, recognition of the emotional nature and appeal of religion; and, secondly, sympathy for the concrete, the historical, the positive, and, above all, the social aspects of religion.

It belongs to the nature of religion, he says, that "it interests the heart."[6] A "cold reason" (*kalte Vernunft*,[7] *kalte Verstand*[8]) will inevitably do injustice to the demands of the life of the imagination (*schöne Phantasie*[9]). Theology and religion are contrasted as *Sache des Verstandes* and *Sache des Herzens*,[10] or as objective and subjective religion. "Objective religion can be arranged in one's head, can be brought into a system, set forth in a book or in a discourse; subjective religion expresses itself only in attitudes and actions. When I say of a man that he is religious, I do not mean that he has a knowledge of it, but that his heart feels the activity, the awe and presence of the Godhead; he sees God in his nature, in the fortunes of men, he bows before Him, utters thanks and praise."[11]

A conscious opposition to the Enlightenment philosophy and those dominant elements in Kant which are expressions of the Enlightenment, mingles with and modifies Hegel's acceptance of the moral religion of Kant. "Wisdom is something different from Enlightenment, from reasoning, for wisdom is not science; it is an elevation of the soul which through experience and reflection has become independent of mere opinion and the impressions of sense. When it is really practical wisdom, not self-complacent or boasting wisdom, it is accompanied by a quiet warmth, a gentle fire. This practical wisdom does but little reasoning, does not

---

[5] It should be noted that Kant's philosophy of religion admits considerably more of the historical and the concrete than he is usually given credit for. Troeltsch has pointed this out in his monograph, *Das Historische in Kant's Religionsphilosophie*, Kantstudien, 1904. However, I shall use the expression "non-Kantian," as the most convenient one to indicate those elements which Hegel opposes to the dominant *Aufklärung* motives of Kant.

[6] Nohl, p. 5.

[7] Nohl, p. 5.

[8] Nohl, p. 8.

[9] Nohl, p. 5.

[10] Nohl, p. 9.

[11] Nohl, p. 6.

proceed *methodo mathematica* from concepts and.arrive at what it takes to be the truth through a series of syllogisms, such as Barbara and Baroko. It has not purchased its convictions at the common market-place where anyone who can count out his money can purchase knowledge . . . but this practical wisdom speaks out of the fulness of the heart.''[12]

   But with these warnings not to forget that religion is a real inner experience, a concern of the heart and the feelings, Hegel does not lose sight of the stern demands of the moral reason. Indeed, these non-Kantian elements of imagination and feeling are insisted upon for the sake of a more real *Vernunftreligion.* Only by thus allying reason and morality with imagination and feeling can Kant's ideal become socially and practically real, a genuine force in human life, a true *Volksreligion.* A *Volksreligion* is to mediate between the Kantian purely moral religion and dogmatic, positive religion.

   This incipient mild mysticism of Hegel is profoundly modified by the second of the non-Kantian elements. This is the interest in the concrete, the historical, and the social. It is not indeed insignificant that Hegel concerned himself with the need and demands of a *Volksreligion,* a religion which within the limit of a definite, historical situation will at the same time embody the essential features of the Kantian *Vernunftreligion.* A true *Volksreligion* will appeal not merely to a universal reason, and to the feelings and emotions of the individual, but will also have a social function, for religion is the sanctifying bond of the common social interests of a definite community; religion is the expression of an historical social consciousness.

   There are thus three factors which so far have emerged in Hegel's thinking. An account of the complete outcome of the interplay of these three factors would be an account of the Hegelian philosophy: reason, immediate experience, and historic life. The Kantian universal reason and formal categories are to enter into immediate experience, and they are going to take on the still more real and concrete form of historic and social life. Hegel's mysticism is to be a social mysticism, where the values immediately realized by the individual in his own feelings, the

---

[12] Nohl, p. 15.

life which he mystically shares, is the concrete life of a real historic epoch, of a people, a true *Geist.* The concept of *Leben,* the central concept of the later mysticism, is here foreshadowed. Immediate feeling, and social historic values unite to form the concept of *Leben.* Here in these earlier fragments, we note the first beginnings of the concept.

It is the task of a *Volksreligion* to "create and nourish the spiritual unity of a people (*den Geist des Volks zu bilden ist zum Teil auch Sache der Volksreligion*). Religion shares this task with political institutions. A true *Volksreligion* gives dignity and significance to the common interests and participations of men. Such a religion goes hand in hand with freedom."[13] That is, the popular concrete institutions of a people, as free expressions of the *Geist* of that people, have a significance which the Kantian and Enlightenment rationalism could not accord them.

The actual historic religious life which embodies for Hegel such a *Volksreligion* at its best is that of classical Greece. There was the perfect blending of *Geist* and freedom, of concrete social interests and reason, of inner pious devotion and adequate public expression and ceremony. The great religious festivals of Greece are the embodiments of such social interests consecrated to the mysterious and the divine.

The comparison between Greek religion (idealized as a true *Volksreligion* because it organized both the Kantian and the non-Kantian elements into a living unity) and Christianity, occupies much of Hegel's attention throughout these fragments. In striking contrast with Greek religion, Christianity is lacking in just those social bonds which characterize Greek religion. The human, the concrete, the social, in short, all that is essential to *Leben* [the word is not here used], is foreign to Christianity. In Chrstianity, as well as in the Jewish religion out of which it developed, the center of gravity is in another realm, to which the natural social interests—those which the Greeks idealized—are foreign.

Christianity was originally a private, personal religion, concerned with the individual's escape from the social misfortunes which oppressed him, instead of absorbing his own in the public

---

[13] Nohl, p. 27.

interests; it was not, like the Greek, an imaginative portrayal of
the mysterious yet joyful common life. Hence the unworldly
(in the bad sense), the melancholy, the oriental aspect of
Christianity. Moreover, after Christianity becomes transformed
from a private religion into a public, political force, its ceremonies, suitable for a private religion, lost their meaning and
their spirit, and never became "socialized with the spirit of joyful
living (*nicht mit der Geist der Fröhlichkeit verbrüdert.*)"[14]

There is that about Christianity which seems to be imposed
from without, constrained and harsh. Compare, for instance, the
imaginative excesses of Christianity and those of Greek religion.
In Christianity there is the morbid, unwholesome imagination of
the tortures of the next world, a detachment from the natural
sober interests of life; but "when the Greek Bacchantes became
aroused to the pitch of madness, saw the Godhead face to face,
and were excited to the wildest outbreaks of a reckless orgy,
there was nevertheless an inspiration of very joy, of enthusiasm,
which once more returned to and entered into the common life
(*eine Begeisterung die bald wieder ins gemeine Leben zurück-
kehrte.*)"[15]

Here was the appeal which the idealized Greek religion and
culture made both to Hegel and to the romantic longing for
completeness and perfection. Here was the realization of all the
motives of which Hegel is thus far conscious. However, Hegel
is not yet willing to make the break with Kant and allow these
non-Kantian elements full sway. He seeks, rather, to reconcile,
and to show the real identity of the formal demands of a pure
reason with the concreteness of life. Thus, love itself, which is
a supreme characteristic of a *Volksreligion,* is in some ways
analogous with reason; "just as love discovers itself in others,
or, rather, forgetting itself and sundered from itself, is active in
another, so it is with reason, which recognizes itself as a principle of universally valid laws and also dwells in each rational
being, as citizen of an intelligible world."[16] But in making this
analogy Hegel is really going beyond Kant. The Kantian

14 Nohl, p. 49.
15 Nohl, p. 54.
16 Nohl, p. 18.

dualism of reason and desire, intelligible and sensible, is on the point of breaking down. A little later, Hegel will be conscious of this and of his opposition to Kant. For here is Kant's intelligible and transcendental world exemplified in the world of human social relationships. Moreover, here is in substance an historical interpretation and transformation of Kant's idealism, which opposed the sensible and the intelligible to each other as two worlds. Once the intelligible world of reason and morality is thus taken historically and humanly, it becomes a growing world of moral and religious values, of what is later called *Leben.* The intelligible world of freedom and morality is to be transplanted from the transcendental and timeless sphere to a natural and human environment, enveloped with mystical feeling. This is precisely the significance of the historical spirit as opposed to a barren metaphysical spirit.[17] Needless to say, the later Hegel became enmeshed in a metaphysical web of his own, and did not remain true to these more modest yet more significant intuitions of his youth.

It is not too much to say that the study of Greek religion, the sympathy for an idealized, free, imaginative religion, which inspired so many of his contemporaries, more than anything else led Hegel ultimately to break away from the Kantian worship of reason. Or, at any rate, it made Hegel see that reason is useless when abstract, distant, and formal, and that the demands of the abstract and the universal must be reconciled with the demands of the concrete, the historical, and the living. The idealized Greek religion was the earliest expression of a concrete universal.

There are thus far two main reasons why Hegel has admitted these non-Kantian motives in his thinking, motives which are to culminate in his subsequent period of mysticism. These reasons are, on the one hand, the study of historical values and experiences such as he believed he found in the idealized world of Greek antiquity. On the other hand, the pathway from the Kantian philosophy of religion to mysticism is not a long one; it may even be called abrupt. Once it be admitted that no

---

17 On the close connection between the romantic and the mystical, on the one hand, and the interest in historical values, the historical spirit, on the other,—a connection not sufficiently appreciated,—cf. Windelband, *Die Philosophie im Deutschen Geistesleben des xix. Jahrhunderts*, p. 36.

knowledge of reality and of the deeper sources of human personality is possible for the theoretical reason, one may fall back on a kind of experience which is of higher validity for knowledge than discursive thought, an attitude and experience of mysticism.

For several years, Hegel concerned himself with another aspect of this problem of the relation between universal reason and the concrete interests of men. It is the problem of the relation between the rational *Vernunftreligion* of Kant (to which, in the main, Hegel still adhered) and the positive, historical religion of Christianity. In the middle of the decade, Hegel writes that he is making a renewed study of Kant,[18] and for a while it seemed as if he were steeping himself more and more in the Kantian way of thinking, and had abandoned the non-Kantian elements of his earlier fragments. His *Life of Jesus* is thoroughly Kantian, more so, in fact, than anything else that he ever wrote. And shortly after his *Life of Jesus,* he wrote the *Positivity of the Christian Religion,* also in the Kantian spirit. But this latter work contains decided hints of both of the non-Kantian elements which appear in the earlier fragments.

In the *Life of Jesus* Hegel interprets the life and teachings of Jesus in the spirit of Kant, and still more in the spirit of the *Aufklärung.* Jesus taught a purely moral religion; he taught that in the doing of one's duty, and in obeying the rational demands of the categorical imperative, man fulfills his destiny and asserts his membership in an intelligible world of reason. Everything in the teaching of Jesus and in the four Gospels that does not illustrate this message is left out of account. The fourth Gospel is used as an historical source for the life of Jesus together with the first three Gospels, but no mention is made of any of its more profound or more mystical implications. Hegel omits in his *Life of Jesus* the analogy between love and reason, and thus the discovery of a more concrete and real reason in the experience of love, which he had formerly hinted at in the *Volksreligion* fragments. Hegel has apparently now accepted in full the Kantian interpretation of religion, and only those elements in the Gospels which can be so interpreted are significant for him here.

---

[18] Letter of Jan., 1795, to Schelling. Cf. *Briefe von und an Hegel,* p. 10.

The *Life of Jesus* was finished July 24, 1795. By November 2, the greater part of the *Positivity of the Christian Religion* had been written. So close together are these two that they may be regarded as forming together a single task. Out of this task, which is historical in its nature, is to grow a conception of religion which breaks once for all with the Enlightenment and Kant. But for the present it is as if Hegel were anxious to see precisely what the purely moral religion which Jesus taught did accomplish, historically and socially. In fact, Christianity became a positive religion. The very failure of the purely moral religion of Jesus to maintain itself as an historical reality may show that after all such a religion is abstract, and does not express all that a religion ought to express. These historical studies of Hegel to gain an insight into the inner life of Christianity and Greek religion, the discovery that a religion conceived in bare terms of the Kantian moral doctrine does not adequately express the demands of that inner life, this it is that brings on the movement to mysticism at the close of the decade.

Jesus undertook, then, to "elevate religion and virtue to morality" among a people who, in their subjection to formal, external laws, knew nothing of moral autonomy and freedom.[19] Jesus himself had no intention of founding a positive religion, based on authority and external sanctions. Any religion is positive whose determining ethical conceptions are founded on heteronomy. What, now, was it, either in the circumstances of the time, or in the form of the original teaching of Jesus, that transformed his purely moral religion first into a sect, and later into a positive faith? This is the historical problem which Hegel here sets himself.

There is another question which Hegel also has in mind, and which is derived from his continued interest in and admiration of Greek religion. His study of Greek religion showed him, as we have seen, a religion which permeated all the tasks and interests of life, and organized them into a spiritual unity. Here, in ancient Greece, was a true *Volksreligion.* Hegel thus comes to see that religion is more than *Vernunft* or morality, as Kant conceived them. What are the reasons that prevented Christi-

---

19 Nohl, p. 154.

anity from becoming such a true *Volksreligion* (as the Greek religion was), and turned it aside into the external, positive, authoritative form which historic Christianity took on?

There was in the very way in which Jesus, as a child of his race, was compelled to utter his message that which soon led to misunderstandings. Jesus was compelled to describe his teachings as the will of God, as if their sanction consisted in their derivation from a supernatural authority instead of from reason. So destitute of genuine moral autonomy were his countrymen that in no other way could they be made to listen to his message. Moreover, Jesus could not neglect the fact that all of his followers were full of the Messiah idea, and would inevitably invest him with at least some attributes of the expected Messiah. Of course, Jesus would and did give to all of this popular expectation just as much ethical emphasis as possible. But he could not disregard it, and the outcome was that the person and the message of Jesus became sundered. More and more his followers looked to the person and the miraculous deeds, and not to the rational teachings, as the essential thing. Even his immediate disciples lost sight of the real ethical and religious teaching, and became absorbed in a one-sided interest in his person; they renounced all of their common interests, political and social, and became simply followers of a man. On the other hand, "the friends of Socrates had from their youth up developed all of their powers in a many-sided way; they had absorbed the republican spirit, which gives to a man more independence and makes it impossible to be merely the follower of a person. For them, it was still worth the trouble to concern oneself about the affairs of the state, and such an interest could never be given up. Most of them had studied under other philosophers and had other teachers; they came to love Socrates for his virtue and his philosophy, and not his virtue and his philosophy because of him."[20]

    As a result of thus misappreciating the actual teaching of Jesus, first a sect, and later a virtual political body based on authority, came into existence as the embodiment of Christianity. What in the early days was a simple and spontaneous commemor-

---

[20] Nohl, p. 163.

ative common meal became later a religious rite invested with
supernatural mystery. The Lord's Supper, which in a few years
Hegel is to regard in a very different light, he now says "became
a religious duty, a mysterious act of religious worship,"[21] lacking in spontaneity and autonomy. The result of all this is that
"Christians have come to just the place where the Jews were,—
slaves under a law."[22] Even the experiences which one ought
to have are prescribed in advance,—one's emotions, one's feelings, one's conversation. How unnatural is all this, how different
from the Greek spirit and the Greek religion! Thus it has happened that the religion which gave the best promise of answering
the demands of morality and reason has turned out to do just
the opposite, to insist everywhere on authority, on form, on
organization, on force; in short, it has become a positive religion.

But the solution of this historical problem is now not enough.
Back of it all in Hegel's mind is the very practical question
which we have seen hinted at in the earlier fragments, a problem
suggested by the idealization of Greek religion: How can a
religion be so constituted as to satisfy both the moral requirements of reason and the concrete requirements of history and of
life? Greek religion did that. Here in this essay, the answer
that Hegel gives shows that the non-Kantian motives in his thinking have become more important. The Kantian reason needs to
be supplemented by the imagination of social values and by the
feeling for them; it must be nourished by concrete social loyalty.
But all this is still made to fit the frame of Kant's rationalism
and purely moral religion.

Any religion which is to be socially adequate will imaginatively embody the ideals of a people, and will associate those
ideals with heroes, with great national personalities who appeal
to the imagination and typify the national aspirations. "These
heroes do not live by themselves, isolated, but in the imagination
of the people; their history, the memory of their deeds, is bound
up with public festivals, temples, works of art."[23] Christianity
has uprooted all these embodiments of national imagination, and

---

[21] Nohl, p. 169.

[22] Nohl, p. 208.

[23] Nohl, p. 214.

in their place has presented us with biblical heroes, strange to us, who do not typify our social and national ideals. Is not this, indeed, the disease from which the modern Protestant world is suffering? It has no heroes and no great common causes that appeal to the unified loyalty and imagination of a people, and hence no true *Volksreligion.* Modern Protestantism, with few exceptions, has not succeeded in its social task of building up a joyful social *Geist,* in which the limitations of isolated and separate personality are overcome, and which is symbolized by a spontaneous, imaginative religious life. ''One could, by dwelling within its walls for a year, almost learn the history of the city of Athens, its culture and its legislation, by watching its religious festivals.''[24]   Instead of a healthy, social imagination which strengthens the community loyalty, the world of *Geist,* the Protestant imagination has emptied itself in a crude superstition. The ideal of the imaginative extension and idealization of the values of concrete social experience, the ideal whose presence and life constitutes the very kernel of religion, has faded away from Protestantism.

The category of *Geist* first emerges, then, as a religious concept. In the world of *Geist* there is the union of a rational and autonomous life with a life full of concrete social interests; and the bond of union is a supreme religious loyalty. In the world of *Geist,* the individuals obey a law of their own making, in obedience to which each loses his private separate self and gains a social self. ''The idea of his fatherland, of his state, was (for the Greek) the invisible, the higher idea for which he labored and which bore him along. This was the final world-goal which was set for him, or, rather, which he was to help set up and attain. In the light of this idea, his separate individuality disappeared; he concerned himself only for the preservation, the life and the upbuilding of that (*i.e.,* the public idea). To ask for or think of his own individuality, his continued existence or everlasting life, could not occur to him, or could but seldom; only in passive and inert moments could he entertain a wish which concerned only himself. Cato turned to Plato's *Phaedo* only after what had been for him the supreme order of things, his world,

---

[24] Nohl, p. 215.

his republic, was destroyed; then he took refuge in another world."[25]

But the imaginative reconstruction and appropriation of the values of history and social life must be spontaneous, and cannot be transferred from one nation to another, or even from one period to another. Hegel, unlike Hölderlin, refused to dwell for long in the ideal world of ancient Greece, satisfied with the contemplation of those distant and departed values. Any attempts to restore the old Greek mythology, or the old Teutonic mythology, hoping that they will satisfy the present social needs, are entirely vain.

Hegel at this juncture can at any rate appreciate the motive of Romanticism, which demands an imaginative life adequate to the inner needs of men. When spontaneously directed to noble national and social ideals, imagination and enthusiasm are legitimate. When the nation is socially bankrupt, where a realm of social values has not been achieved, where there is no solidarity of *Geist,* then imagination and enthusiasm will run riot, not held in check and ennobled by social loyalty. This, in short, is Hegel's relation to Romanticism. He appreciates the motive, he sympathizes with the needs of imagination and enthusiasm, he sees their effectiveness for religion and a developed social consciousness; all of this has come from his sympathetic study of Greek religion. But he insists that all of this should serve the purposes of reason, of autonomy, and of the concrete social interests. There is much in common between this sympathy on Hegel's part for noble and imaginative idealizations of the common aspirations of a people and the romantic enthusiasm over the life of the Middle Ages, amounting to its idolization; as, for instance, in Friedrich Schlegel and Herder, the latter of whom undoubtedly influenced Hegel not inconsiderably.[26]

Why did the Greek religion, with so much in its favor, a real *Volksreligion,* disintegrate and succumb to Christianity,, with its positive teaching? "How could a religion disappear which for centuries had made itself a power in the state, which was most intimately bound up with public life; how disappear faith in

25 Nohl, p. 222.
26 Hegel refers to Herder by name, page 218.

gods to whom was ascribed the founding of cities, to whom men
brought daily offerings, whose blessings were invoked for all
enterprises, under whose banners alone armies were victorious,
whom men thanked for their victories, to whom were offered
both the songs of joy and the prayers of piety, whose temples,
whose altars, whose wealth, whose statues were the pride of the
people and the glory of art, whose worship and whose festivals
were but the occasion of universal joy,—how could the faith in
such gods, faith woven into the tissues of human life with a
thousand strands,—how could such faith be rooted out?''[27]
This is a description of that *Phantasiereligion* of Greek culture
which no Enlightenment philosophy could ever understand. Such
a philosophy supposed that the light of reason led men to see the
grotesqueness and contradictions of their myths and fables, and
to accept a rational form of Christianity. But ''whoever has
made the simple observation that the heathen who believed in
such fables also possessed understanding, that they are our
masters in all that is great and beautiful, noble and free, . . .
whoever knows that a religion, and especially a *Phantasiereligion,*
is never banished from the heart and the whole life of a people
by cold reasoning which you elaborate in your study; whoever
knows, further, that in the spread of Christianity something very
different from reason and understanding was used, . . . such
an one will never rest content with this answer.''[28]

Hegel discovers the reason for the displacement of the Greek
Phantasiereligion by the Christian positive religion in the social
and political changes which brought the ancient world to a close.
Religion is an imaginative reflex of the social spirit of a people.
Nowhere does Hegel show the advance he has made beyond Kant
more than in this recognition of the significance of historical
and social movements. A broadly social interpretation of history,
in terms, that is to say, of social psychology, of the animating
Geist of a people,—an economic interpretation of history where
''economic'' means social, moral, and spiritual economy as well
as financial,—this is Hegel's earliest conception of a dialectic of
history.

---

[27] Nohl, p. 220.
[28] Nohl, p. 221.

Applying this general conception to the problem in hand, Hegel's answer is that "the Greek and Roman religion was a religion only for a free people, and with the loss of their freedom, the meaning, the power and the suitability of their religion must also have been lost. The prime reason for this loss of freedom is economic and political; wars and the increase of wealth and luxury led to aristocracy and to inner decay. Loyalty and freedom, the joyous participation in a common life, all disappeared."[29] "All activity, all purposes were now referred to individuals; no more was there an activity for the sake of a totality, for an *Idee*."[30]

But the center of gravity of a man's life, the directing goal of his activities, must be found somewhere. "Reason could not renounce the hope of finding somewhere the absolute, the independent, the practical."[31] Life is impossible without loyalty. But after the break-up of the Greek social institutions, which, while they lasted, did furnish such a center of gravity, the Greek gods and Greek religion could not supply the want. Those gods, —and this had been their true strength and their title to worship, —had been imaginative symbols of social institutions and values, and became worthless after the disintegration of those values and institutions. "In this condition, without faith in anything abiding, anything absolute; in this yielding to a foreign will and law; in an unhappy state which made itself felt only through its oppression; in a worship of the gods to which men could bring no joy, . . . in this situation a new religion offered itself to men. It was a religion which was either already adapted to the exigencies of the time because it had arisen amongst a people suffering from a similar emptiness and want; or, it was a religion out of which men could form that which their needs demanded."[32] The result is a positive Christianity where the ideal, the center of gravity, is made remote and transcendent, instead of immanent in the realm of human social values and experience.[33] It follows

---

[29] Nohl, p. 221.

[30] Nohl, p. 223.

[31] Nohl, p. 224.

[32] Nohl, p. 224.

[33] Dilthey has pointed out that this is essentially a portrayal of the stage of "das unglückliche Bewusstsein" in the *Phenomenology*. *Jugendgeschichte*, p. 36.

that the good, the ideal, can now only be wished for, not wrought out and elaborated in the natural world. The world became estranged from itself, impotent to develop and realize ideals from within. Another result of all this is the Christian doctrine of original sin and the depravity of man.

The most important characteristic of this world now thoroughly at odds with itself is that which explains the Christian conception of God as a transcendent entity, an object, a substance. Thus Hegel says: "The despotism of the Roman emperors had driven the spirit of man from the earth, the loss of freedom compelled him to rescue his eternal, his absolute, by taking refuge in the Godhead (*der Raub der Freiheit hatte ihn gezwungen sein Ewiges, sein Absolutes, in die Gottheit zu flüchten*)."[34] God becomes a mere object, just in proportion as men lose their moral autonomy and become slaves. The need of some other category than that of *Object* adequately to express God as he lives in the life of a free people, is the upshot of this discussion. This is the doctrine of the *Phenomenology*, that the category of Substance must yield to that of Subject. Hegel learned this from his insight into the living, free *Phantasiereligion* of the Greeks. Hegel's mature doctrine, that in some sense God and the universal consciousness of the Church are one, that God exists through the consciousness of those who worship him, is thus shadowed forth in this early study of the contrast between the *Phantasiereligion* of the Greek world, and the positive Christian religion which has degraded God into an external, wonder-working and authoritative Substance.

Thus far, in the earliest *Volksreligion* fragments and in this account of the Positiveness of the Christian religion, Hegel has been studying the possibility of the purely moral religion of Kant fulfilling those demands which he is more and more appreciating. These are the demands of feeling, of immediate experience, on the one hand, and the demands of social and historic values on the other. It is the appreciation of an idealized Greek culture, which Hegel shares with the prevalent romantic spirit, and of the place in that culture of social loyalty and enthusiasm, which leads him to see the inadequacies of Kant's position.

---

[34] Nohl, p. 227.

And now Hegel is to break completely with Kant, and give
full swing to these non-Kantian motives. He does this in a series
of writings which Nohl has grouped together under the title of
Der Geist des Christentums und sein Schicksal. Nohl decides
that these writings belong to the last two years of the decade.[35]
In these writings there is a singularly clear expression of motives
which are everywhere those of mysticism; there is the emergence
of something like the later dialectical process; there is a new and
more profound interpretation of Christianity; and the entire
thought of this group of writings centers around the explicit
category of *Leben.*

A remarkable portrayal and criticism of the spirit of the
Hebrew religion forms the introduction to this new interpretation
of Christianity. Accompanying this criticism is a running comparison between the Old Testament and the Greek religion. The
Hebrew religion from first to last was the religion of a people in
conflict with themselves and with nature, of a people who were
not at home in their universe, and who never developed any
capacity to love and to live.

The story of the flood witnesses to the belief in a profound
disruption between man and nature. At the end of the flood
there was no true reconciliation between man and nature, but
instead a "peace of necessity" which could but prolong the feud.
How different is the Greek story of Deucalion and Pyrrha who,
"after their flood undertook to recall mankind to friendship for
the world, to nature. To make them forget stern necessity and
hostility through joy and happiness, they concluded a peace of
love, thus became the ancestors of glorious nations, and made
their age the mother of a new-born nature which should preserve
its youthful spirit."[36]

The first recorded act of Abraham is his leaving his fatherland, his ancestral home. "The first act through which Abraham
became the ancestor of a nation was an estrangement (*Tren-*

[35] Rosenkranz and Haym do not bring these writings together, and they
place them in the earlier Bern, rather than in the later Frankfurt period. It
is the most important result of Nohl's critical editorship that we can regard
these wrtings as forming something of a unity, and as coming after the
earlier writings of the Bern period, which are very much more in the spirit
of Kant.

[36] Nohl, p. 245.

nung) which tore asunder the bonds of the common life and love, all the ties which had formerly bound him to man and nature,—those beautiful ties of his youth he now cast from him. Cadmus, too, and Danaus, left the fatherland, but they set out to find a place where life and love could grow. Abraham had no desire to love and hence be free. These, Cadmus and Danaus, in order to live in undisturbed beautiful relations (which they could no longer do in their own land), carried their gods with them. Abraham desired release from just these ties. Cadmus and Danaus, through their graceful art and manners, attracted the natives to themselves, mixed with them, and became a happy and joyous people. Abraham and his people were always hostile to their neighbors, determinined to maintain a rigid opposition to everything (*der Geist sich in strenger Entgegensetzung gegen alles zu erhalten*). . . . He was a wanderer and a stranger upon the earth. . . . But love did not exist for him (*nur lieben konnte er nichts*). Even the only love which he had,— that for his son—he was willing to sacrifice."[37] The flight of the Hebrews from Egypt was a cowardly flight, animated by no genuine longing for freedom, no loyalty to their common life. "The Jews conquered, but they had not fought; the Egyptians were vanquished, but not by their enemies."[38] And the liberator of the people freed them only to lay upon them a new burden, that of the Law. Here, again, the whole basis of their legislation was the "opposition and estrangement between themselves and the infinite Object to whom they accorded all truth and reality. The remoteness and barrenness of the ideal and the divine center of their life, their Deity, is expressed in the sacred aloofness of their Holy of Holies. How different at Eleusis, where the divine was poured out among the people and revealed in countless images, emotions, words and thoughts! But, for Israel, the divine was ever external, unseen and unfelt."[39]

The most human thing about the Hebrew religion was the yearly feasts, for undoubtedly here would be life; on the other hand, how empty and void of life is the Sabbath, lacking in the

37 Nohl, p. 245ff.

38 Nohl, p. 249.

39 Nohl, p. 251.

cultivation of all human interests. Complete abject passivity here, no life! After satisfying the formal demands of their slavish religion, there is nothing left for the Hebrews to do but physically live. Nothing spontaneous appeared to sustain and glorify their natural interests. It follows that no truth about God is to be found in the Old Testament, but only commands. Truth is always something free. "That upon which one is dependent cannot have the form of truth; for truth is beauty imaged by the understanding, and the negative characteristic of truth is freedom. (. . . *das von dem man abhängig ist, kann nicht die Form einer Wahrheit haben; denn die Wahrheit ist die Schönheit, mit dem Verstande vorgestellt, der negative Character der Wahrheit ist Freiheit).*"[40] In this earliest Hegelian definition of truth, used here to discredit the truth of a religion and theology which is entirely lacking in aesthetic beauty and life, Hegel shows considerable sympathy with the romantic temperament.

All the successive misfortunes of the Jewish people are nothing but the consequences and developments of this their primitive fate, their complete estrangement from nature, and their slavish dependence upon the God who should have been instead the ideal and imaginative embodiment of complete freedom and life. "The great tragedy of the Jewish people is no Greek tragedy; it can awaken neither sympathy nor fear, for these emotions arise only when a thoroughly beautiful nature is broken by stern fate. This Jewish tragedy can only inspire abhorrence. The fate of the Jewish people is the fate of Macbeth, who cut himself off from all nature, formed strange ties, and in this strange service bruised and murdered everything sacred in human nature, and finally, abandoned by his gods (for they were mere objects and he a mere slave), was himself destroyed."[41]

The message and the fate of Jesus are only intelligible when seen upon this background. Jesus set himself resolutely against the whole spirit of this people. The fundamentally new insight into the nature of religion which Hegel presents in these fragments is this: The religious values and experiences of any life,—

---

[40] Nohl, p. 254.
[41] Nohl, p. 260.

and Life, *Leben,* is more than the separate existence of finite individuals,—consists in the development and healing of differences in that one life, and imaginatively representing as the ideal the one completely unified life: not, as in Judaism, setting up a complete opposition between our concrete life and interests and an external authoritative object. "Since religion is the most spiritual thing, the most beautiful thing, the thing which strives to unify the oppositions latent in any development, and which represents the unification as complete in the ideal and no more estranged from reality, and since religion seeks to express and strengthen that complete unification in deeds, it follows that any religion which lacks this spirit of beauty is the very emptiest thing imaginable. It is the most servile slavery, which implies a consciousness of its nothingness, and demands something in which man expresses his not-being and his passivity. Even the satisfaction of the most common human want is elevated above this, sees more to life than this; for it possesses at least an interest of some sort, however empty."[42]

The concerns of the one life, the common life shared in by all, are of supreme significance. No law, even though it be a law of reason, can prevail against it. Life is more than reason. That which one experiences in the welling up and unification of this one life cannot be adequately expressed in terms of so abstract a category as reason. This is the essence of Hegel's mysticism of this period, and of his departure from Kant. Or, to express it in terms of another category which is here emerging and used with great frequency, the category of *Begriff,* one might suppose with Kant, and with Hegel himself during his earlier Kantian period, that the task of Jesus was merely to state the moral law in terms of autonomy rather than heteronomy, as the universal law of one's own reason and moral will. Such an autonomous universal law is a *Begriff.* But merely to do this would be only a partial achievement; "by such a process the positivity or heteronomy would be only in part done away with."[43] One would now be a slave to a merely universal law. The merely universal is always abstract, is never able to do justice to the

---

[42] Nohl, p. 262.
[43] Nohl, p. 265.

concrete and the living, is never able adequately to express its nature. "The universal is always and everywhere hostile to, and objective to the particular, to impulses, to concrete interests, pathological love, sensibility."[44] No, the spirit of the teaching of Jesus is in another sphere, one which transcends the oppositions of abstract morality. The Sermon on the Mount, which Hegel had previously interpreted in the Kantian fashion, is now interpreted in this new mystical way. That which takes one beyond the abstract universal *Begriff*, or *Sollen*, is *Life*, "*ein Sein, eine Modification des Lebens.*"[45] An immediate experience of this *Leben*, of the Spirit, overcomes the opposition, heals the breach which abstract reason creates and cannot heal. Hence, it is not a new command which Jesus substitutes for the Old Testament law; that his utterances take on the form of a command is due to the fact that the living experience, or spirit (*das Lebendige*), is subjected to thought, is spoken, takes on the form of a *Begriff*, a form which is external to its real nature. Not commands, nor *Begriffe*, but *das Lebendige*, a spirit and a life on a higher level than any which reason and discourse can comprehend. In this life the thought of duty disappears. This higher level of spiritual activity possesses an immediacy, a concreteness, a *Sein*, which closes the chasm between subject and object, impulse and law; and "at this higher level the moral law loses its abstract universality, and the subject (the impulse or desire) loses its sundered separateness."[46] It is an experience for which the ideal is not foreign and merely an object of thought, but one which in its own immediacy and activity shares in the life of the ideal. The category wherewith to express this confluence, this mutual sharing of the universal and the particular, of the moral law and the concrete interest, is that of *Leben*.

In the most important of the fragments now before us, and probably the most important single thing written by Hegel before the *Phenomenology*, there is a union of the various concepts and threads which we have thus far been following. In this fragment now to be taken up there is a culmination of Hegel's mysticism,

---

[44] Nohl, p. 266.

[45] Nohl, p. 266.

[46] Nohl, p. 268.

an interpretation in terms of this mysticism of the central doctrines of Christianity, and above all, the background of his later system and his dialectic.

It is once more from the idealized Greek culture that Hegel borrows a concept wherewith to solve the problem which the self-estranged culture of the Old Testament and the Kantian morality both present. For the Kantian philosophy leaves one with a problem instead of a solution. Here once more is the problem. If the sharp sundering of the universal, unyielding law and the concrete living interests of men be maintained, then when the law is violated, when sin is committed, there is no possible means of bringing about a reconciliation. The law must take its course, and punishment must follow as a mathematical necessity, as a mechanical reaction of the disturbed system. "So long as law is the highest category, just so long is there no escape, and so long must the individual be sacrificed to the universal, the law; the life of the individual must be destroyed."[47] So long as this regime of universal law holds sway, one person can in no way represent others, and atone for their sins. Each human being is a separate atom, a mere particular, when viewed in the light of the abstract universal. How can this antagonism, this hatred between the external overpowering force of the law, which has been violated and demands retribution, and the particular impulse and life be reconciled? The Greek concept of Fate (*Schicksal*) effects this reconciliation. For, when the punishment comes as the act of Fate, and not as the retribution of Law, it does not stand forever above and against you as a sheer universal; it is merely a hostile force coming against you, individual and concrete just as you are. It is but one current of the universal life meeting your current, and this clash is set in motion by your misdeed. The entire process of sin, of injury, remorse, punishment, and reconciliation goes on *within the total Leben,* and is not the collision of *Leben* with an external ought. For notice, the sin which an individual commits is a wound (*Trennung*) somewhere in the tissue of this universal *Leben,* and wounds can be healed. Since all Life, all Spirit, is one, and is a totality, the wrong-doer comes to see that through his wrong he

---

[47] Nohl, p. 278.

has really injured his own life, and not merely violated an external law. He has wounded this One Life; has introduced a separation within his own real life. "The wrong-doer supposed that it was but an external foreign thing that his sin affected; really he has but torn asunder his own life. For no life is separate from Life, because all life is divine and of God. The wrong-doer has in his wantonness, to be sure, done damage,— but it is the friendliness of Life which he has injured; he has made it an enemy. . . . Thus his punishment, regarded as his fate, is the return of his own deed, a force which he himself has set in motion, an enemy of his own making. . . . It seems far more hopeless to expect a reconciliation with this Fate, than with the Law; for, in order to become reconciled with Fate, it would appear necessary that the injury itself should disappear. But Fate has the advantage over an external Law, because with Fate, the entire process goes on within *Leben*. A wrong-doing in the Kantian realm of law is in the realm of irreconcilable opposites, both of which are fixed realities (*unüberwindlichen Entgegensetzungen, absoluter Wirklichkeiten*). There is no possibility here of transcending the punishment or of allowing the consciousness of having done wrong to disappear. The law is a power, to which all *Leben* is a slave, and to which there is nothing superior, for God himself is but the giver of the law. . . . *Leben* can heal its wounds, can bring back to itself that sundered, hostile life which the wrong-doing caused to split off; can atone for and sublate the bungling work of the wrong-doer, the law, and the punishment. From just the moment when the wrong-doer feels the wounding of his own life (suffers punishment), or is conscious of his life as sundered and bruised (in remorse), then the working of Fate has commenced, and the consciousness of the wounded life must also be a longing for its restoration. The lost life is now appreciated as his own, as that which should now be his, but which is not. This gap, this void, is not a mere nothing, but it is actively known and felt as the lack of life. To think of this Fate as possible is to fear it; but this is a different fear from the fear of punishment. It is the fear of self-estrangement and loss of self; the fear of punishment is the fear of something merely foreign."[48]

---

[48] Nohl, p. 280.

Another name for this healing is Love (*diese Vereinigung ist in der Liebe*).[49]   Life is restored to itself through Love (*das Leben hat in der Liebe das Leben wiedergefunden*)." This feeling of Life which once more finds itself is Love, and in Love Fate is reconciled and atoned for."[50]   It is in the fact that the opposing force is felt to be one's own life, that the possibility of becoming reconciled with it lies.

Two remarks may justify these extended quotations. First, this movement within the one universal *Leben* is of a dialectical nature, and foreshadows the dialectic of the future system. Secondly, this mystical way of interpreting the shortcomings, the sins of finite individuals, means an advance beyond the Greek religion. To be sure, the concept of Fate is taken from Greek tragedy, but the type of experience portrayed is not Greek but Christian. Hegel has here discovered an experience, a life, which possesses an inner self-movement; a spirit, that may fairly be called dialectical. The very life of this experience consists in an overcoming of opposition, a winning of peace, an atonement and reconciliation through sin and conflict.

That the Hegelian Dialectic, when it is first discovered and noted, is a movement of life, and not a movement of logic, is significant.[51]   It suggests an inquiry as to the dialectic of the *Logic*. Is that dialectic rightly interpreted when it is taken as an extreme form of panlogism, as the self-development of logical concepts which somehow spin out a complete set of logical categories? Or, is the dialectic of the *Logic* an extremely artificial and elaborate expression of certain movements of life, of passion, of moral and religious experience, such as, in a simple case, wrong-doing, remorse, reconciliation, and love? Is Hegel

---

49 Nohl, p. 281.

50 Nohl, p. 283.

51 Dilthey has pointed out that in this process which goes on within *Leben*, a process of tension, separation, and reconciliation, we have the earliest form of Hegel's dialectic of history. Cf. *Jugendgeschichte*, p. 99. It should also be added that this dialectic of life, of history, of *Leben*, is the real dialectic of Hegel. That of the *Logic*, of pure ideas, is a formal expression of the dialectical character of the mystical experience of *Leben* which Hegel here describes. Hegel's insistence in the *Phenomenology* that the consciousness of the forgiveness of sin furnishes the best means of appreciating what religion means, shows that the dialectic of religious and moral experience was then also uppermost in his mind.

after all the great mystic, and one who has attempted a logic of mysticism?

As to the second point, there is something more than a suggestion here that the one universal *Leben* is indeed richer because of all of its wounds, and because of the labor and love of healing them. These sunderings, these expressions of clashing, are, in their totality, the very condition of the exercise of love. Otherwise, all were static sameness, without growth and without life (*denn die Entgegensetzung ist die Möglichkeit der Wiedervereinigung*).[52] The dialectical connection between suffering and love, the oppositions within *Leben* to be overcome,—this it is which the Christian doctrine of the Atonement represents. And this whole conception of *Leben*, Hegel insists, is the central part of the teaching of Jesus. The healing power of love, the overcoming of oppositions, the forgiveness of sin, this is what goes on in *Leben*.

Hegel outgrew his dependence upon Kant and the Enlightenment rationalism, not by discovering logical or metaphysical difficulties in them, but by discovering a type of experience, religious and mystical, for which the Kantian categories of reason are wholly inadequate.[53] That Hegel definitely has broken away from the *Vernunftreligion* of Kant, and that he has come to a mystical interpretation of religion and Christianity, is clearly seen in his discussion of the relation between virtue and love. No real unity of life is possible on the basis of a moral law, of virtue, of reason. Such a unity is abstract, cannot mediate between the conflict of interests in a growing society. Such a unity is a mere thought-product, a mere concept (*nur ein Gedachtes*), and not a living bond. Something higher than reason holds life together and gives it significance. Virtue is on the level of reason; love is on the higher level. Such a spirit of love, a feeling for the whole of Life (*Empfindung des Ganzen*), cannot be commanded, and it transcends rational definition. No mere virtue or abstract universal can grasp it; it is no mere "unity which a concept possesses, but an inner harmony of the spirit,

---

[52] Nohl, p. 282.

[53] It is just this mystical type of experience which seems wholly paradoxical from the standpoint of sober common logic (*Verstand*), and which thus demands a new logic. Cf. Dilthey, *Jugendgeschichte*, p. 172.

godliness; to love God is to feel oneself without bounds, absorbed in the universal Life of the Infinite (*nicht eine Einheit des Begriffs, sondern Einigkeit des Geistes, Göttlichkeit; Gott lieben ist sich im All des Lebens schrankenlos im Unendlichen fühlen*)." "Kant's Practical Reason, with its merely abstract universal, leaves life really disorganized; the concrete is excluded and not absorbed (*Kant's practische Vernunft ist das Vermögen der Allgemeinheit, d. h. das Vermögen auszuschliessen; . . . dies Ausgeschlos ene in Furcht unterjocht—eine Desorganisation, das Ausschliessen eines noch Vereinigten; das Ausgeschlossene ist nicht ein Aufgehobenes, sondern ein Getrenntes noch Bestehendes*)."[54]

In the living experience which transcends the external morality of Kant, Hegel notes three stages. They are: an inner disposition (*Gesinnung*), love, and religion. These are three stages in a single developing experience, which grows by overcoming and transcending previous shortcomings,—a dialectical process. The realm of the teaching of Jesus is that of *Gesinnung* and *Liebe*. *Gesinnung* is a disposition, which in a particular case, brings desire and the moral law into harmony. But this is limited, and apt to be sporadic. It becomes universal and constant only when *Gesinnung* is elevated to *Liebe*. But this does not end the process, for love is not religion. In an outline which Hegel wrote, and which is printed as an appendix by Nohl,[55] Hegel mentions the three great limitations, shortcomings, in the Kantian morality and in the Old Testament. These are, first, the chasm between man and the law (*Willenslosigkeit*); secondly, the chasm between man and man (*Gefühlslosigkeit, Mangel schöner Beziehungen*); and, thirdly, the chasm between man and God. Not until this third chasm is bridged over and healed by religion is the final stage reached. Love is not yet religion, and does not become such until it is imaginatively and mystically presented to the mind, until it transcends the limits of separate persons, and becomes more objective, more real, and in a sense more metaphysical, than mere private feelings of love. Hence the Last Supper was a true love-feast, but not a strictly religious rite. For "it is only a

---

54 Nohl, pp. 295, 296, 388.

55 Nohl, p. 386.

bringing together and harmonizing in love, which is made objective by the imagination, that can be the object of true religious reverence.''[56]   In the Lord's Supper, the bread and the wine are only transient symbols.   What constitutes the essence of religion is the mystical and imaginative apprehension of a perfect unity, which contains all life and love.   ''Love is a divine spirit, but not yet religion.   To become such, it must take on an objective form; a subjective sensation must fuse with something presented and universal, and thus win the form of a significant Being, worthy of worship.   This need, that of uniting the subjective and the objective, of bringing together immediate experience and the demand for the objective, the understanding,—the need of uniting all of these through the imagination into a thing of beauty, into something Divine, a God,—this is the impulse to religion.''[57]   In the mystical apprehension and recognition of this Divine, of *reines Leben*,[58] one has transcended the love of one's fellowmen.   This universal divine life transcends our human finite life, but in the religious experience here portrayed we share in this one divine life, which is thus nothing foreign or hostile.

Hegel now clearly expresses, over and over again, what he has hinted at from the very first emergence of non-Kantian motives, and what is the kernel of all mysticism.   *Reines Leben,* this mystical level of experience, cannot be grasped or comprehended by thought and understanding.   Moreover, the categories of substance and personality are therefore entirely inadequate to express the true nature of this *reines Leben.*   ''Since the Divine is pure Spirit (*reines Leben*), it follows that nothing can be asserted of it which involves mutual opposition; all expressions of reflection concerning objective relations or concerning objective ways of acting must be avoided here.   For the activity of the Divine is naught but a union of minds, and only Spirit can comprehend and do justice to that which is Spirit.''[59]

The chief interest of mysticism, here as elsewhere, lies in asserting the necessity of going beyond the categories of discursive thought, of reflection, which deals only with objects, and

---

[56] Nohl, p. 297.
[57] Noh, p. 332.
[58] Nohl, p. 302.
[59] Nohl, p. 304.

opposing to this something higher and more immediate. Here in these writings, the opposition is that between *Reflection*, or *Verstand*, and *reines Leben*, or *Geist*. In the *Phenomenology* and the *Logic*, it is the opposition between *Verstand* and what purports to be a different and higher type of thought, *i.e.*, *Vernunft*. But the real nature of the opposition remains constant. What Hegel's later philosophy attempts is the working out of the logic of this experience which transcends discursive reason. Hence, the dialectic, the life of the *Logic*, is in its intention and spirit a survey of the way in which this higher type of experience develops; it is a logic of what may fairly be called the experience of mysticism. *"Über Göttliches kann darum nur in Begeisterung gesprochen werden."*[60] The *Logic* and the *Phenomenology* are attempts to make such spiritual *Begeisterung* articulate. Such is the light which these early writings throw on the "Rationalism" of Hegel. The Rationalism of the later Hegel concerns only the form. Hegel's *Logic* unites the matter of mysticism and the form of rationalism.[61]

We come now to Hegel's mystical interpretation of Christianity. The poverty of suitable concepts in the religion of the Jews compelled Jesus to use for his mystical insight wholly inadequate expressions. Moreover, the Prologue of the fourth gospel, and the mystical discourses of Jesus in that gospel, are not really logical propositions, giving information, substances, objects, things external and abstract. "These assertions have only the illusory appearance of being logical propositions; for their predicates are not concepts, universals, which is the case in judgments of reflection. Here the predicate is something immediate (*seiendes*), spiritual, and living (*lebendiges*). Simple reflection is not fitted to express the essence of the spiritual."[62] To attempt to express the relation between man and God, and

---

60 Nohl, p. 305.

61 The opinion, then, that Hegel has nothing of the mystic about him (Cf. Haym, *Hegel und seine Zeit*, p. 58, "*der mystische Zug seinem Wesen von Hause aus fremder ist*") needs decided modification. Rosenkranz is far nearer right. Cf. *Hegel's Leben*, p. 58, "*Dem kritischen und skeptischen Geist in ihm stand ein im guten Sinne des Wortes mystischer gegenüber, aus welchem er sich über den Standpunct der blossen Moralität in der Religion erhob.*" But Rosenkranz does not recognize how intimate the relation is between this mystical intuition, and the core of the later system.

62 Nohl, p. 306.

man and man, in the form of propositions, is to sunder an immediately experienced spiritual life (*Zerreissung des Lebens*). This relation can be set forth only mystically (*nur mystisch gesprochen werden kann*)."[63] Again, "The connection between the infinite and the finite is a sacred mystery, just because this connection is Life itself (*der Zusammenhang des Unendlichen und des Endlichen ist freilich ein heiliges Geheimnis, weil dieser Zusammenhang das Leben selbst ist*)."[64] "Understanding, reflexion, always results in separateness, opposition (*absolute Trennung, das Toten*)."[65] Herein lies the true interpretation of faith. Faith transcends knowledge; when faith is completed, it signifies a conscious recognition of the unity of the Spirit, a *Ruckkehr zur Gottheit*. "*Gott kann nicht gelehrt, nicht gelehrnt werden, denn er ist Leben, und kann nur mit Leben gefasst werden.*"[66]

This doctrine of the immediacy of the world of *Leben* further implies that the category of substance, of object, even though it be a person, cannot be used within this realm, to describe the living unity of the Spirit. God, the infinite *All des Lebens*, the Totality, is not external to the finite parts. "The whole is external to the part, is beyond it as an object, an outlying substance, only when one is talking of dead objects; in the Spirit, on the contrary, the part is as truly a unified totality as the whole. When the particular finite parts are conceived as substances, although each is taken together with all its properties as an individual, their common nature, their unity can then be only a concept, not a living essence (*nur ein Begriff, nicht ein Wesen, ein Seiendes*). But in the case of spiritual beings, they possess reality, true immediate being, even when separate, and their unity is just such an immediately apprehended nature." Is it a contradiction to say that the part is as truly a unified totality as the whole? No, "for what exists as a contradiction in the realm of the dead, *i.e.*, of mere objects, is not a contradiction in the realm of Life (*Was im Reich des Toten Widerspruch ist, ist*

63 Nohl, p. 308.
64 Nohl, p. 309.
65 Nohl, p. 311.
66 Nohl, p. 318.

es nicht im Reich des Lebens).''[67]   This is indeed the keynote of
the system and the *Logic.*

Faith in a person is but the first stage. To be mystically
united with the divine is more than merely to have faith in a
divine person. This mystical union could not be fully realized
until Jesus should depart, and the last element of objectivity and
externality should disappear. This means a transcending of the
category of personality. The first disciples of Jesus could not
separate his person from the spiritual life which they now had.
They were still in the stage of *Glauben,* of faith in another
person, not of union with the universal divine life itself. The
communion of the church becomes the visible symbol of this
mystical union. This is the Kingdom of God, now interpreted
mystically, instead of ethically, as Hegel had previously done.
''This living harmony of men, their common life in God, Jesus
now calls the Kingdom of God.'' The common bond of this
mystical society is not an abstract rational law of morality, a
mere *Begriff,* but ''love, a living bond.''[68]

But there is another story which now needs to be told. This
mystical religious ideal and life could not endure. Christianity
became positive. The life gradually disappeared and religion
became once more limited by the category of substance, instead
of having freedom through the mystical category of spirit. God
again becomes an object instead of a life; religion becomes metaphysical. This is Hegel's attempt to show how the metaphysical,
objective God-consciousness of Christian theology was evolved
out of the truer mystical religion of the founder. The religious
community, whose bond of union was to have been the mystical
partaking by each member of the Divine life becomes divorced
from the common interests of men,—the state, the temporal, the
mundane. This means a shrinking of its life and of its own
interests (*Beschränkung des Lebens*). Here, once more, it is the
Hellenic ideal of a free development of all the concrete interests
of life, which is contrasted with the sort of fate which the
Christian religious community was compelled to undergo. It is
the withered and lifeless body of the Jewish spirit, with its

---

[67] Nohl, p. 308.
[68] Nohl, p. 321.

formality and externality, which is responsible for this harsh fate both of Jesus and of the religion founded by him. "Jesus had to choose between sharing this withered and artificial life of his people, but of course sacrificing all the beauty and life of his own spirit, and his union with the Divine; or else of withdrawing entirely from the harsh fate of his people, of opposing his life to theirs,—thus in neither case fulfilling the demands of nature. . . . He chose the latter alternative, the sundering of his own life from the world about him, and this, too, he demanded from his followers." This is the tragedy of his life. He, who cared so much for the life of men and whose very religion consisted in finding God in a mystical appropriation of the love of mankind, and who came thus to provide more abundant life,—he was compelled to renounce whatever life he did come amongst, because it was so barren and outworn. Hegel puts this in a remarkable way when he says that Jesus was compelled to find his freedom in an empty void (*so konnte er die Freiheit nur in der Leere finden*), instead of in a free life within the social institutions of men. Once more it is the Greek ideal of a social consciousness, of common interests, without which there is no religion, no *Leben*. This is the true reason for all that other-worldliness from which Christianity has suffered. The church has feared and shunned all wholesome enthusiasm for the common social interests and tasks of men. A "fear of life" (*Furcht für jedes Lebensform*) "a fanaticism which despises life" (*lebensverachtende Schwärmerei*), is the fate of a religion which intended and hoped to do so much to ennoble and enlarge the interests of life.[69]

This flight from the interests of concrete social life, this forsaking of *Leben* by *Liebe*, and the consequent shrinking of *Liebe*, has had as its most significant consequence the necessity of an *external* bond of union, *e.g.*, an objective God, a deified Jesus, to take the place of the inner, mystical bond of union. This new objective bond must, then, be received from without; it must be, for instance, a common creed, beliefs in historical and external events. "To a really spiritual and living community nothing is given; what the spirit and the living community itself becomes, that it receives." Nothing foreign need come to it. "But the

---

[69] Nohl, pp. 328, 329.

spirit of this love, *i.e.*, that of the church, which has sundered itsel˄ from the concrete life, is so barren, feels itself to be so empty, that it must needs conceive of the Spirit which belongs to it as not really *of* it, not an expression of its own life but as foreign.''[70] Hence· the opposition of God and the world, the sundering of the divine and the human, the setting off of God as a transcendent object. So far has this gone, that it is no longer possible for Christianity to rest content with an ''impersonal living spirit of beauty (*in einer unpersönlichen lebendigen Schönheit Ruhe zu finden*), impossible to bring together into a unity church and state, the worship of God and *Leben,* piety and virtue, spiritual and worldly activity.''[71]

All of this involves, of course, a new interpretation of what is meant in calling Christianity a positive religion. While under the influence of Kant, Hegel understood by a positive religion one in which moral heteronomy prevails, as in the Old Testament. From his new mystical point of view, Hegel understands by positive a religion whose bond of unity is an objective substance, an objective God, instead of a common and universal life, mystically and imaginatively shared. Hegel now calls Christianity a positive religion because it disregards as irrelevant the concrete life which is immediately present in all experience. The representatives of the Enlightenment, for instance Lessing, had drawn the distinction between the rational essence of religion and its historical accidents. They had hoped to use the concept of merely rational human nature as a valid criterion of everything historical and concrete. The result was that nothing historical and concrete was regarded as significant, because it involved something over and above the abstractly rational. What Hegel's social mysticism has taught him is that reality is to be found only where there is concrete life, and that this concrete life can never be extracted or represented by understanding and reason. The result is that at least some elements of what the Enlightenment had thrown aside as mere irrelevant particulars, mere historical accidents, prove themselves to be necessary in order to have any religion at all.

[70] Nohl, p. 336.
[71] Nohl, p. 342.

The few pages which are the beginnings of a working over of tnis question of Positivity are written from this new standpoint of social mysticism. Thus, ''The living nature is always more than the concept; accordingly, what for the concept is a mere modification, a pure accident, something superfluous, may be in reality a necessity, a vital element, perhaps the only truly natural and beautiful element.'' . . . ''The universal concepts of human nature are too empty ever to furnish a standard for the particular and necessarily complicated needs of the religious consciousness.''[72] Hegel is here conscious of the conflict between any account of religion which the rationalism of the Enlightenment could give, and the account which a sympathetic historical insight might give. He now turns to this historical · religious consciousness, and hence the historical interest of this period succeeding the Kantian.

There is foreshadowed just here the doctrine of truth which Hegel develops in the *Phenomenology,*—the doctrine that truth is not a fixed external thing against which our concrete experience must passively measure itself, and to which it must conform, but that the truth and worth of an experience is something won and achieved as an historical development. Christianity became a positive religion, in the bad sense, when it denied the divinity of its own concrete experiences, when it sundered man from God, when it subjected itself to external standards, when it ceased to be mystical and became metaphysical. ''This view of the relation of the Christian religion to mankind is by no means to be itself called positive; it rests on the securely beautiful presupposition that everything in man which is exalted and noble and good is divine, comes from God and is of his spirit. This becomes a positive religion when human nature is sundered from the divine nature, when no mediation exists except in the person of a single individual, and instead, all human consciousness of the good and the divine is debased to a mere sham (*Dumpfheit*) and is extinguished by the belief in something wholly foreign and supernatural.''[73]

I have spoken of Hegel's mysticism as a social or moral

---

[72] Nohl, p. 141.
[73] Nohl, p. 146.

mysticism. I have meant thereby to contrast it with any mysticism for which all concrete and especially all social interests are irrelevant, whose utterance is the *neti, neti,* of the Upanishads, and which issues in a blank negativity. The isolated and wayward character of such mysticism leads to the "unhappy consciousness" which Hegel has portrayed so well in the *Phenomenology*. The mysticism of Hegel as shown in these early writings finds its life in an appropriation and fostering of the concrete life of humanity, and in regarding these values as emblems of a larger and more mysterious unity of *Leben*. The unity of the one *Leben* in spite of, or better, because of, all its disruptions and wounds, a unity which is immediately apprehended in an experience which from the standpoint of common-sense logic seems paradoxical,—this is an integral element in the mysticism of Hegel. But mysticism everywhere has grasped at such a unity, and has attempted some such immediate experience of it. What is characteristic here of Hegel's mysticism is the intimate relation between the one mystically apprehended *Leben* and the historic social consciousness. *Leben* has, throughout, these two aspects: it is a universal life, a unity in which we mystically share; it is also a definite realm of concrete social values which calls for experiential activity and loyalty, a realm of living *Geist*. Hence, *Leben* is characterized by historic development.

It is this union of the mystical and the historical, of these two aspects of *Leben,* which generates the dialectic. Any process is dialectical where there is a pervading unity through a series of *apparently* separate, exclusive, and contradictory events or elements. Such a unity is mystical, because, transcending rational and logical formulation, it needs to be immediately experienced; and it is historical, because there is a development throughout a series of concrete situations which are related to each other as the successive epochs of a single historical process. But in spite of its being in this sense mystical,—transcending rational and logical formulation,—it must work in some definite way and obey some law. Hence, the dialectic is the way in which such a mystical experience is organized, the way in which it develops. This mystical experience is an experience, an intuition, of more unity in the world of ethical and social values, of *Geist,* than appears to a superficial and common-sense view.

Titles in This Series

Adams, George Plimpton, see Gray, J. Glenn

1

Baillie, Sir James Black
The Origin and Significance of Hegel's Logic
(London, 1901)

2

Baillie, Sir James Black
An Outline of the Idealistic Construction of Experience
(London, 1906)

3

Croce, Benedetto
What Is Living and What Is Dead of the Philosophy of Hegel
(Translated by Douglas Ainslie, London, 1915)

4

Cunningham, Gustavus Watts
Thought and Reality in Hegel's System
(New York, 1910)

5

Foster, M. B.
The Political Philosophies of Plato and Hegel
(Oxford, 1935)

6

Gray, J. Glenn
Hegel's Hellenic Ideal
(New York, 1941)

bound with

Adams, George Plimpton
The Mystical Element in Hegel's Early Theological Writings
(Berkeley, California: University of California Publications
in Philosophy, vol. 2, no. 4, Sept. 24, 1910, pp. 67–102)

7

Haldar, Hiralal
Neo-Hegelianism
(London, 1927)

8

Harris, William T.
*Hegel's Logic. A Book on the Genesis of the Categories
of the Mind*
(Chicago, 1890)

9

Hegel, Georg Wilhelm Friedrich
Political Writings
(Oxford, 1964)

10

Hibben, John Grier
Hegel's Logic: An Essay in Interpretation
(New York, 1902)

11

Löwith, Karl
From Hegel to Nietzsche
(New York, 1964)

12

McTaggart, John McTaggart Ellis
Studies in Hegelian Cosmology
(Cambridge, 1901)

13

Niel, Henri
De la Médiation dans la philosophie de Hegel
(Paris, 1945)

14

Stirling, James Hutchison
What Is Thought?
(Edinburgh, 1900)

15

Wahl, Jean
Le Malheur de la conscience dans la philosophie de Hegel
(Paris, 1951)

16

Walsh, W. H.
Hegelian Ethics
(London, 1969)